Milking the
Painted Cow

MILKING THE PAINTED COW

The Creative Power of Mind and the Shape of Reality in Light of the Buddhist Tradition

Tarthang Tulku

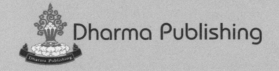

Dharma Publishing

 DHARMA IN THE WEST

Mind Over Matter
Milking the Painted Cow

Library of Congress Control Number: 2004116742
ISBN: 0–89800–368–7

Cover Design by Colin Dorsey

Printed in the USA by Dharma Press

10 9 8 7 6 5 4 3 2 1

To all students of the Dharma.
May your efforts be blessed with success.

Contents

PART TWO

THE CHALLENGE OF STUDYING DHARMA TODAY

PART THREE
DAILY DHARMA

APPENDICES

Preface
Mind and the Three Turnings

The Buddha presented the Dharma in eighty-four thousand topics, a wealth of teachings that is vast beyond comprehension. The scriptural transmission of these teachings is known in Tibetan as lung (Skt. āgama), while the realization of the meaning of the teachings is known as rtogs (Skt. adhigama).

It is essential for new Dharma students to become aware of the vastness and complexity of these teachings. For example, the teachings can be classified in terms of audience, trainings, and content. The three kinds of audience (who follow the three yānas, or vehicles) are the Śrāvakas (Tib. nyan-thos), Pratyekabuddhas (Tib. rang sangs-rgyas), and Bodhisattvas (byang-chub sems-dpa'). The three trainings are śīla (Tib. tshul-khrims): conduct that brings stability and clarity to the mind; samādhi (Tib. ting-nge-'dzin): directing the mind; and prajñā (Tib. shes-rab): training in wisdom. The three sections or 'baskets' (tripiṭaka, sde-snod gsum) into which the teachings can be organized are Vinaya, Sūtra, and Abhidharma. Simply stated, the three baskets of the scriptural transmission instruct us in how to apply the three trainings that orient the mind to the Dharma and lead to realization of the meaning of the teachings (rtogs).

To explore this great treasure-house of knowledge, it is important to understand something of the historical development of Buddhism. After Śākyamuni, the fourth Buddha of this era, had fulfilled the path that frees beings from the illusions and confusion of samsara, he resolved to guide others to liberation. This act of boundless compassion initiated a living lineage of realization. Two major transmission streams for the Dharma developed. One was handed down by great Arhats such as Śāriputra, Maudgalyāyana, Ānanda, Subhūti, and Kāśyapa. The second traced through the great Bodhisattvas: Maitreya, Avalokiteśvara, Mañjuśrī, Vajrapāṇi, Samantabhadra, Kṣitigarbha, and others.

The teachings transmitted through these living lineages all have in common a focus on mind. In countless ways and with countless methods, they ask how mental activity arises and functions and how to analyze, educate, and transform the mind. Whether the issue is the ālaya (Tib. kun-gzhi) as the foundation for experience, reality and illusion, the workings of karma and kleśa, or the stages of samādhi; whether the method is philosophical analysis, meditative inquiry, logic, or empirical investigation, mind is always the subject at hand.

Mind embodies the causes and effects of karma (Tib. las) and kleśa (Tib. nyon-mongs), and karma and kleśa in turn are manufactured by mind. Another way to say this is that mind generates illusion and reflects illusion. An ancient image describes this mind of illusion as an armless rider on a blind stallion. The horse is deluded ignorance, charging off oblivious in all directions. Lacking any way to control mind's energy, awareness is powerless. Led by the mind of illusion, sentient beings are carried ever deeper into samsara.

How the Teachings Fit Together

The beginning Dharma student should never forget that the central practice of investigating and transforming mind can be conducted in different ways and at different levels. Terms such as consciousness, conception, perception, cognition, and interdependent cooperation (Skt. pratītyasamutpāda, Tib. rten-'brel) are each assigned different meanings depending on their application in different aspects of the teachings, different schools, and different texts. Consistent with the basic focus on mind, they are interpreted differently to serve different purposes.

For instance, the Śrāvakas and Pratyekabuddhas emphasize the application of antidotes to karma and kleśa. They investigate the causal chain that links one mental event to the next, forming the patterns of illusion mind, and they aim to break the chain through practice of the three trainings. Bodhisattvas emphasize understanding how mind itself arises and how it fabricates samsara. In their practice of the three trainings, they aim to transform the mind of illusion directly into enlightened awareness, revealing samsara itself to be illusory.

These different emphases can be linked to the classification of the Buddha's teachings into Three Turnings of the Wheel of Dharma. First-Turning teachings focus most closely on the Vinaya and the Abhidharma, while Second- and Third-Turning teachings rely on the Sūtras.

The First-Turning Vinaya rules of conduct teach how to emulate the enlightened way of life. The Vinaya overcomes self-centered desire, bringing calm and stability to the mind through conduct that accords with śīla. Relying on the protection of Vinaya, members of the eight kinds of Sangha live free from fear: like a yogin serene in a desert overrun by scorpions, they know that samsara's poisons cannot harm them. Once cultivated by eighteen schools of Buddhism, the practice of the Vinaya continues today in the lineage of Rāhula transmitted by the Sarvāstivādins and in the lineage that traces to Kāśyapa, continued within the Theravādin tradition.

The First-Turning teachings of the Abhidharma cultivate prajñā. With scientific objectivity and precision, they analyze the operations of samsaric mind, clarifying the workings of karma and kleśa, the defilements, the Four Truths, and interdependent cooperation. As therapy for the ills of samsara, Abhidharma overcomes ignorance. It identifies fifty-one mental events and analyzes their functions, their interactions, and their consequences.

Abhidharma is a vast subject, but today only a few key texts remain. For the Mahāyāna, the main works for studying Abhidharma are Vasubandhu's Abhidharmakoṣa and its Bhāṣya—commentaries known as the lower Abhidharma—and Asaṅga's Abhidharmasamuccaya, known as the higher Abhidharma.

The teachings of the Second- and Third-Turning Sūtras lead to the vastness and profundity of complete and perfect enlightenment. The Prajñāpāramitā teachings of the Second Turning emphasize the penetrating depth of understanding associated with śūnyatā (a term related to the nature of reality), while the Sūtras of the Third Turning present the quality of illumination (Skt. prabhāsa, Tib. 'od-gsal) within śūnyatā. Revealed in dialogues with the Bodhisattvas Avalokiteśvara, Mañjuśrī, and Maitreya and the Arhats Subhūti and Śāriputra, the Second and Third-Turning teachings have guided countless Bodhisattvas toward realization. The depth of the Second-Turning teachings was explored by Nāgārjuna and his followers, including Āryadeva, Buddhapālita, and Candrakīrti.

The vastness of the Third Turning is expressed in the treatises of Maitreya. Maitreya transmitted these teachings to Asaṅga, who passed on his realization to Vasubandhu and others, founding a tradition of great siddhas and yogins.

The meditative practices of śamatha (Tib. zhi-gnas) and vipaśyanā (Tib. lhag-mthong), common to all Buddhist traditions, bring calm to the wild energies of mind and clarify the confusion created by ignorance, so that mind no longer unceasingly accumulates karma and kleśa. Visualization can deepen this calm, and certain samādhis can transform illusion mind completely. When meditative mind gains independence from illusion mind, it becomes possible to follow the teachings truly.

Perhaps this book can serve some readers as a guide toward developing such independence. It grew out of dialogues with students over the past few years, dialogues that center on the theme of how traditional teachings can guide the efforts of our community as we work to lay a foundation for a Western Sangha. Thinking to present a brief overview of a few fundamental points, I gave some notes to Jack Petranker, who expressed my thoughts in these essays. My daughter Pema Gellek requested that information be included about traditional teachings, which she helped prepare. I gave additional notes to Leslie Bradburn, who edited the material.

It has been more than thirty years since I settled in the West, and during that time I have worked very hard. In one sense, I have found my work enormously profitable, more so than if I were a bank president or wealthy entrepreneur, for I have been able to invest the West's vast material resources on behalf of knowledge and the Dharma. I have done so with the wish that through such efforts the Dharma may flourish for a long time to come.

My thanks and deep appreciation go to this land of opportunity and religious freedom, and especially to my helpers and to our long-time friends and supporters. I can say with conviction that the blessings of

Guru Padmasambhava and my lineage will reward the goodness and kindness you have shown for the past three decades. I can only hope that the next generation—my own children, our friends, and younger students—will carry forward what we have established. I wish them all success. There is a future for the Dharma in this country, and they have a role to play in its creation and unfolding.

PART ONE

Getting Clear
on Mind

*The Buddha's teachings can be summarized
in four statements (sDom-pa bzhi):*

All that is compounded is impermanent.
All that is defiled with emotionality is suffering.
All dharmas are empty.
Nirvana is peace.

Responsibility for Mind:
How to Start Dharma Practice

The intentions and understanding we manifest as individuals are crucial in shaping the state of the world we live in. The self-centered hopes and fears of the individual are the building blocks of the conflicts between nations; our inner disharmonies are reflected in imbalances between humanity and nature. Imagine a world where minds were open and free of suffering, where peace was possible and harmony inherent. Such a world would be a paradise indeed, an enlightened realm where wisdom and compassion ruled.

Any progress in that direction is surely worth the effort, for the benefit of ourselves as well as others. So it is important to be clear at the outset that whatever progress we make in this direction will come entirely through deepening our understanding of mind. The beautiful flower of human transformation, a vision of possibilities, grows from the muddy water of each moment of ordinary experience. The Dharma shows how this can happen.

Serious study of Dharma begins with the recognition of the centrality of suffering in our experience and with a wish to understand how it comes about. This wish leads directly into the topics of karma and kleśa—the behavior patterns and emotionalities that give mind's fabrications their momentum and sustain our steady refusal to see through what mind presents. Ultimately it shows us the need to understand the causes of our ignorance.

When we turn our attention toward karma, kleśa, and ignorance on this basis, we engage them not as philosophical issues, but as forces that seem to run our lives. Yet this is not an easy thing to do. Even though we see suffering all around us, it is very difficult to accept the truth of suffering. It is even harder to realize that we are somehow responsible for it, through our engagement of karma, kleśa, and ignorance.

We can understand more about suffering and ignorance by considering the first of the sDom-pa bzhi, the Four Statements that summarize the Buddha's teachings: All compounded things are impermanent. Applying this statement to ourselves and our own situation requires special effort, since we seem to go on in the same way from day to day and year to year. Of course we will admit there have been changes, but 'we' are the same—the child, the adult, the old man or woman are all 'me'. The evidence of impermanence is right before us, in the changing of each moment of experience in this ever-changing realm, but our vision is not attuned to its manifestations. We recognize change at certain mid-range levels of space and time, but not at the micro and macro levels. We do not feel the planet moving; we do not see our cells changing.

We do see our bodies grow old and our hair gray, so our ignorance cannot be complete. Conceptually we have to agree that all that is born will one day die. But somehow we persuade ourselves that the 'all' does not include 'me'. Intellectually we say yes, but emotionally we say no. We simply are not convinced that one day we will be gone, although it is completely and utterly certain that this so. This not-seeing is ignorance. It runs very deep.

Taking ourselves as permanent, behaving as if life will continue forever, we think, feel, and act in ways that would change radically if we were vividly aware of our own transience. This ignorant believing in self-permanence obligates us to take certain things very seriously. It sets up a belief system that intimidates us and prevents us from acting with clarity. We hold on tightly to problems, ideas, self-imaginations, and conflicts as if we were somehow obligated to undergo frustration. Although we may know that the harder we hold on, the more intense the frustration becomes, we still cannot let go. The mind remains occupied night and day with various levels of frustration that cannot be released or resolved.

The core belief in the solid permanent self we think we are creates enormous suffering. Once this belief is in place as 'real', a whole array of tasks spreads out before us. Our most pressing job is to make the self feel important, to enlarge the domain of the self, to chase after whatever the self demands, to control, avoid, and remove whatever the self dislikes or fears. It does not seem possible to refuse these emotional commitments we have made to the self. As a consequence, karma and kleśa fill and shape our lives. This situation is not the result of someone's personal fault or idiosyncrasy. It is simply the way of samsaric identity founded on ignorance.

The Buddha taught that the antidote for ignorance is knowledge. If we understand the nature of karma and kleśa and ignorance, if we understand identity and self, then we have completely new choices. If we see through the 'realness' of what is true only in a relative way, if we question the interpretations of mind and let go of the grasping at self-beliefs, we may discover how we have been fooling ourselves. If we can investigate both the self that has been fooled and the self doing the fooling, we may find that samsara is ultimately śūnyatā. The shining sword of wisdom can cut karma and kleśa, transform suffering, banish confusion, and bring the reign of ignorance to an end.

How do we begin the process of understanding and develop knowledge that is the antidote to not-knowing? Where do we start and how do we look? We can see at the outset that the task is not easy. All of humanity wishes to bring suffering to an end, but look how few have succeeded! Science has developed an enormous body of knowledge based on observation of the physical world, but this approach does not yield knowledge that will heal our frustration once and for all, nor does it fundamentally resolve our uneasiness at being a self.

The process of enlightenment discovered by the Buddha takes a different approach. It points inward, identifying mind as the master of samsara and nirvana. If the process of observation that science cultivates is expanded to include mind as well as matter, we have taken the vital first step toward developing the tools and the methods needed to understand the operation of karma, kleśa, and ignorance.

We have an obligation to ourselves and to humanity to take this step—to take responsibility for our own minds—for the mind is far more influential than matter. The most powerful material forces, such as weapons of war or miraculous medicines, originate with intentions of mind. Even horrific natural disasters, far beyond our power to control, can be viewed as important lessons or transformed into human triumphs through the mind's creative power.

To activate the power of mind, Dharma practice begins with the Four Foundations of Mindfulness: body, feelings, mind, and Dharma. Through mindfulness, calm and insight (śamatha and vipaśyanā, zhignas and lhag-mthong) gradually develop. Like the wings of a bird, these two work together to carry the practitioner through all the stages of the path.

In practicing the Four Foundations of Mindfulness, students begin with the first three: attention to body sensations, feelings, and the thoughts that run through the mind. Over time, gentle, relaxed attention to what is happening in body and mind gives rise to calm and stability, the ability to be present with experience. In the light of mindfulness of Dharma teachings, such as impermanence, selflessness, and suffering, the mindfulness of body, feelings, and thoughts stimulates the development of understanding, preparing for further progress. That is why the Four Foundations are said to be the first four of the Thirty-Seven Wings of Enlightenment, the comprehensive practices that together make up the Buddhist path. Practiced with diligence, they lead to the beginning of the end of ignorance, opening a way of wisdom that leads through the Five Paths and the Ten Stages to the complete and perfect Enlightenment of the Buddha.

Manifestations of Mind:
How Can Mind Be Trained?

Mind manifests an infinite capacity for self-expression: angry mind, greedy mind, selfish mind, resentful mind, or lusting mind; suspicious mind, proud mind, ignorant mind, opinionated mind, noisy mind, intense mind, or mind that is made up; critical mind, picky mind, assertive mind, biased mind; foggy mind, bored mind, lazy mind, procrastinating mind, lost mind, cloudy mind; unreliable mind, unpredictable mind, changeable mind, unstable mind, chaotic mind; self-loathing mind, guilty mind, paranoid mind, envious mind. There is also joyful mind, peaceful mind, kind mind, or loving mind. There is caring mind, thoughtful mind, positive mind, affectionate mind, wholesome mind, compassionate mind, awakened mind; generous mind, disciplined mind, patient mind; energetic mind, contemplative mind, and wise mind.

Like the artist painting, the chef cooking, or the chemist mixing up poison or medicine in the laboratory, mind creates experience. Just as space exhibits the whole of the material universe and the fabric of our lives, so mind manifests all experience and all appearance. We live 'in' the mind. We ourselves are the body of mind, the process of mind.

Our well-being depends on mind, for the power of mind is undeniable. Illusion mind can lead us into spirals of depression, circles of confusion, or stagnant pools of indifference. Meditation mind can lead to the joy and equanimity of the samādhis. Awareness mind can forestall mistakes and lead us toward virtue, joy, compassion, and effortless effort. Mind can be our best friend, supporting us in every difficulty, or our fierce enemy, turning even simple acts of perception into occasions for devastating suffering.

The Buddha taught that illusion mind is deeply unreliable. Changeable, emotional, and confused, illusion mind cycles endlessly through samsaric rhythms of joy and misery, boom and bust. Whatever it identifies as significant or trustworthy will prove disappointing; whatever methods it sets in place will work poorly or fail completely.

Because the body of mind is so unstable, the character of mind is difficult to catch. Knowingly, we do not wish for confusion, but unknowingly we actually create and sustain it. Mind is devious and defensive, demanding and determined not to obey. If challenged, mind turns to emotional dramas that exaggerate or denigrate or to radical intellectualizing that asserts unquestionable limits: "This cannot be done because of that; that cannot be done because of this!"

The very changeability of mind is a sign that mind is trainable. If we can learn something from mind, we might be able to teach mind and transform it. We might gain control over mind, so that we do not need to follow its every mood. The Buddha's wisdom was born from gaining complete access to the nature and dynamics of mind. If we could follow in his path, we too might win freedom from illusion mind. But our knowledge is always directed at appearance as it arises within a specific realm, and so it has no way to understand the one that has already programmed that realm—mind! Without access to new ways of knowing, we will always find ourselves already engaged in the ongoing dynamic of the current realm. We can only affirm that predetermined way of minding.

A first step in understanding illusion mind is to recognize just how this dynamic works—how mind programs experience. Some forms of psychology or religious practice work extensively at this level of insight. They set out to teach the mind to program certain kinds of experience. But Buddhism takes a different approach. It analyzes how mind generates and operates the programming itself—how emotional qualities and reactive ways of acting bind us to limited, repetitive ways of being—and goes on to investigate the body and foundation of mind. The All-knowing Buddha could see the structure of our illusions and how they arise, and he passed that knowledge on to his followers. The same knowledge is available to us today.

The Enlightened One taught that we can use the capacities of illusion mind to turn from samsara and follow in his path. Practicing awareness of experience as it arises, we can progress from the level of words and concepts and ordinary experience to a transcending, awakened awareness that engages knowledge differently. This higher, intrinsic, all-knowing knowledge the Dharma symbolically gives the name prajñā. But in fact it is beyond naming, beyond the senses, and beyond thinking—beyond all activity of illusion mind. The path for students of Dharma is to embody prajñā, relinquishing old ways of knowing and being, moving eventually beyond training and transforming to transcendence, where mind itself becomes śūnyatā.

Approaching the Mind:
How New Knowledge Can Be Found

Slippery and elusive, mind continually streams in different directions. Sometimes it instructs, investigates, and comments; sometimes it directs, perceives, and makes distinctions; sometimes it manipulates and judges. Sometimes it reacts to what is perceived; sometimes it appears as the background of specific perceptions. Whatever concepts or words or ideas we apply to take hold of it, mind will extend beyond them.

It may seem we could leave concepts behind and investigate mind through direct experience, but this is far from easy. Experience arises as feelings, thoughts, and impressions interact with consciousness to label and identify appearance. Meanings arise from dialogues that depend on mental imagery and sense perception. All this is the activity of mind. Since it is mind that narrates experience, experience as such cannot lead us to understand mind.

Buddhist practice and analysis suggest that the way to investigate mind begins by training mind. The method for doing so is the three trainings. śīla, samādhi, and prajñā. Training in śīla makes disciplined conduct a path of inquiry into the operation of karma. As exemplars of śīla, the Sangha demonstrate that mastery of karma is possible. Śīla leads to samādhi, which is not captured by the kleśas and so engages mind differently, preparing the way for pra-jñā. Investigating the samsaric structures of mind, pra-jñā guides meditation more deeply into the samādhis.

Working in harmony, the three trainings give access to new kinds of input, not based on 'minding', that support new forms of practice. Through the inte-gration of refined conduct, the transformations of samādhi, and penetrating analysis the kleśas give way, and the bhūmis of the Bodhisattva path come within reach. Now prajñā matures to investigate the relation between reality and appearance. Entering countless samādhis, Bodhisattvas traverse the stages of the path. They dwell in worlds different from the world of ordinary existence, each with specific obsta-cles, attainments, and ways of transcending. Drawing on mind's creative power, the Bodhisattvas employ extraordinary mental capacities and faculties. Through their growing mastery of mind, they perfect śīla, samādhi, and prajñā and increasingly exhibit the qual-ities and actions of the Kāya, Vaca, and Citta of the Enlightened Ones.

The Play of Mind

Until the three trainings take hold, illusion mind unfolds with a steady momentum, establishing what seems real. The Western mind, fascinated with drama —television and movies, novels and plays—is familiar with this momentum. It knows how readily fictions engage the mind, provoking reactions that feed the ongoing momentum. Even so, Western understanding scarcely suspects that its own daily dramas operate in a similar manner, a magical display generated through the rules and roles of the prevailing fiction.

As the instrument for sorting out experience in meaningful ways, mind works a most distinctive magic. Out of an initial translucent awareness, fundamental roles are assigned: telling and told, creator and creation, and the temporal baseline along which the play of appearance unfolds. Against the background of what is already established, mind classifies, categorizes, and establishes patterns, relying on core distinctions such as right and wrong or real and not real. Caught up in mind's rhythms, perceptions are structured by pre-existing attitudes and understandings that feed back to perception the expected, like a familiar face reflected in a mirror.

Pointing out appearances, mind demands a response, and mind itself complies by identifying and distinguishing what is so: birth and death, dream and reality, conscious and unconscious. Playing out this reality, we apply tests for what is real, but since the tests emerge out of the same momentum of mind as what is tested, they only confirm what mind has presented. As the particularity of each perception is identified in terms of the generality of what has already been set in place, language, concepts, and meanings proliferate. Just as the media feed on stories created by the media, triggering accelerating cycles of change, so within mind each thought, each feeling, each layer of consciousness has its own momentum that contributes to the shape and integrity of the whole. Each new formation becomes a component of another, more complex formation that further verifies the overarching reality—the story of the self.

Like clouds in the sky, illusory mind is constantly shifting shapes. Some new story is always taking form: the scientific version, the social version, the historical version, the religious version, the psychological version, the naive version, the 'natural' version. As patterns, processes, and stories proliferate, the field of mind grows vast. Qualities emerge: beauty, happiness, confusion, emotionality; inspiring virtues and innovative visions. Different forms of knowledge and disciplines of practice take form: art, music, healing; science, religion, psychology, and more. People interact; social and political structures are established. Civilizations rise and fall; whole histories are enacted, set down, and then lost forever. Stars form, blaze brightly, and burn out. The unknown becomes known, and the previously known recedes from view.

Resisting Insight into Mind

In the midst of the mind's fabrications stands the mind-created phantom called 'self'. Through self, mind gives body to mind, assigning a label so that it can point to itself and its activities. Once the name is in place, the self can anchor the operations of mind, thereby confirming its own existence as the actor, the narrator, and the audience of the most convincing story of all. Narrator, actor and audience all interact, initiating dialogues about the way things are. These dialogues add credibility and weightiness to the actor's next act, feeding the momentum it generates and the interpretations that arise in its wake.

Although it seems at first glance the most solid of all mind's fabrications, the self is actually a weak link in the interlocking structures mind sets in place. Analyzed in a therapeutic, meditative way, the self's claim to stand as the enduring entity central to every story proves hard to maintain. And since it is so central, once the self comes into question, the vitality drains out of the whole of what we take to be real. We begin to get a sense of what it means to speak of reality and mind as illusion.

Such insight, however, goes against the momentum that drives the mind's fabrications. So we have learned to hold it at a distance, fearful that chaos and darkness would descend if we saw 'through' our usual perspective.

Intent on security, we rely on the mind's limited ways of viewing, embracing narrow focal settings as 'obvious' and 'clear'. In particular, we single out the perspectives that offer guidance and goals: the pursuit of fame, wealth, power, or pleasure; devotion to art, religion, or skeptical rationality; technology, telepathy, or yogic attainments. Instantaneous transitions are cloaked with summary conclusions: "Now I am happy;" "This is nice;" "That is too difficult." When distinctions cannot be made and identities fail to arise, a sense of dullness and numbness gathers, a not-knowing that corrodes cognition and demands repair. Or a sense of panic overwhelms the mind, domineering in its intensity, insisting that some kind of 'solution' be manufactured.

This deep-seated vulnerability to ignorance and confusion is why Buddhist inquiry depends on the three trainings: śīla, samādhi, and prajñā. Before we can deeply investigate the structures that illusion mind imposes, we must recognize the activity and power of karma and kleśa. Without necessarily following a formal scheme for analysis, such as those of the Abhidharma or Madhyamaka, students can develop self-understanding by stimulating inquiry into mind. Viewing from fresh angles can open up a freer way of seeing. Even when progress is slow, even when the mind shies away from knowledge by hiding in confusion or dullness, we have the opportunity for greater knowledge, for it is just in such reactions that we can catch a glimpse of the mind-fabrication process in action.

The Matter of Mind

Mind's fabrications bind us to samsara not because they are false, but because they trap us in a fixed and limited way of being. When we accept the authority and legitimacy of the regime established by mind, we accept the authority and legitimacy of samsara itself.

We uphold it with each idea we affirm, each word we pronounce, and each experience we claim as our own.

Can we challenge the authority of mind to bind us? Here we encounter a fundamental difficulty. When we look for the body of mind, we find only the clothes that mind wears, a fabric woven by the interplay of senses, thoughts, images, and cognitive faculties. As weaver, mind stands apart from all this. It has no place, no shape or form, no 'from' or 'to'. Then how can we take hold of it or investigate it? Like the finger that cannot touch itself, mind seems beyond the reach of any mental operation. But if mind is unknowable, how can we call it into question?

Mind's stories seem to confirm the existence of mind as storyteller. A certain experience has arrived, so there must be a mind to experience it. But this is just another story. Mind readily reports on its own activity, the senses recognize themselves in the images they generate, and consciousness cognizes its own features in the meaningful structures it imposes. But none of this takes us outside the stream of stories. As the stream flows along, each 'popping up' and then subsiding, we may experience a 'field' of mind and its accompanying 'feel', seemingly more basic than the content of any particular story. Yet even these forms of evidence depend on stories told by the mind: stories of experience, stories of logic, stories of temporal succession and causal sequence.

If we cannot contact mind apart from the ideas and interpretations it puts forward, could we speculate that mind does not exist at all—that the clothes have no emperor? What if mind is like the anchor on a television news program, coordinating and introducing the stories reported on that day's broadcast? The anchor, like the reporters who narrate each story, is simply a part of the broadcast: there when the show begins and gone when it comes to a close. Likewise, when mind's presentations cease, the evidence for mind disappears.

But this kind of speculation is simply not true to our experience. When we are caught in pain and suffering, or have to decide, or stumble into confusion, mind is very real. As long as samsara is real, as long as there is a self to suffer, mind will continue to run our lives, no matter what intellectual arguments we advance to undermine its legitimacy. Mind is not matter, but mind does matter. That is why looking into mind means investigating what seems to matter most of all.

The real difficulty may not be that we have no access to mind, but that mind is something so different from what we imagine that it requires a completely different way of investigation. Consider as an analogy a strange fact about our knowledge of the physical universe. Scientists sometimes claim that the periodic table of the elements and the laws of subatomic physics give them a comprehensive understanding of all the matter in the cosmos. Yet the available evidence, viewed in light of our current understanding of the laws of nature, strongly suggests that ninety-five percent of the substance in the universe is 'dark matter' or 'dark energy', invisible to all our observations and measurements. What can this mean? Perhaps one day we will find that the universe is composed of radically different particles or forces than we now imagine, elements that can be discovered only through a whole new set of approaches, theories, and methods of inquiry. Could the same be true of mind?

Questioning Mind

The great masters of the Mahāyāna set forth various conceptual analyses that can lead toward new kinds of knowledge. Nāgārjuna in his Mūlamadhyamaka-kārikā and Candrakīrti in his Prasannapadā present a Sevenfold Reasoning (saptavidyā, rnam-bdun rig-pa) that questions the persons and things that make up our everyday conventional truth (saṁvṛti-satya, kun-rdzob bden-pa). Taking a chariot as an example, one would analyze in the following manner:

> Is a chariot inherently the same as its parts, such as axles, wheels, seat, and frame?
>
> If not, is a chariot inherently different from its parts?
>
> Does a chariot inherently depend on its parts?
>
> Do the parts inherently depend on the chariot?
>
> Does a chariot possess its parts?
>
> Is a chariot the collection of its parts?
>
> Is the chariot the shape of its parts?

We can apply these same seven questions to the body. Is the body the same as, or different from, its parts (arms, legs, head, torso, etc.)? We speak as if there is a foundation that holds the parts together, some basis for the word 'body'. But if the body were the same as the parts, how could we take away an arm and still have a body? If we imagine that each of the parts is taken away one by one, at what point do we say the body is no longer there? The same analysis can be extended to the next level of structure. Is the arm the same as the bones, joints, skin, muscles, etc. that make it up?

Once we conclude that the body is not the same as its parts, we ask if the body is different from its parts. Can a body be observed that is separate from its parts? Have we ever seen a body without any parts? If there are many parts, does this mean there many bodies?

Similarly, we can examine the self in relation to the body. Is the self the same as the body? Is it different from the body? Is the self the same as the mind? Is it different from the mind? How does it stand in relation to the elements making up mind, such as feelings, perceptions, impulses, and consciousness? Performing such an analysis in careful detail changes the raw naiveté that would never think to question the existence of the self. If the self is not the same as or different from the mind or body, not dependent or independent of them, not the possessor or the overarching whole, then where is it and what is it? When we see that this self we have taken for granted is difficult to pin down, our questioning deepens. We might see "where our head is at" in a surprising way.

If we grow suspicious enough, we might find ourselves asking whether the self is an illusion, the product of some kind of self-created magic. The mind is convinced the self is real. Is it mind that creates this sense of identity and goes on to convince itself? Is there a self apart from mind? Suppose that there were: How could we define and identify such a self?

When we use the sevenfold reasoning on the self, it may seem that we are attacking the self. But that is not the point at all. Instead, it is important to articulate clearly what we think about self and mind and how they connect. When we do this examination for ourselves, we can see what our underlying ideas are, whether they make sense, and how they might be questioned further. Liberating thoughts may arise, elevating our way of thinking and exerting a meaningful influence on our perception of self-identity.

It is important to get clear on how important the story of the self is to our ongoing experience. Once there is 'I', 'mine' arises, establishing possessions or territory of the self. With these two perspectives in place, all the operations of mind come into play. They create subjective experience: the full range of human emotions and thoughts, from the depths of despair to the heights of elation, with all the suffering and happiness of everyday life in between. This is the stuff of everyone's life-story, 'the story of myself'. Though the chapters take unexpected turns, and chapters already completed may be rewritten, the basic identity of the main character is not questioned. We are completely certain there is an owner, a knower, an enjoyer, a controller, a seeker, and a finder—and that one is 'me'.

These identities 'make sense'. They feel comfortable. In contrast, non-identity seems like untenable non-sense. It offers no orientation, and it feels profoundly uncomfortable. But as we learn more about the 'who' we are dealing with and how reliable this 'who' is, we may get a glimpse of the 'how' of this 'who'—how mind and self work. This is a fundamental discovery, or rediscovery. Making contact with this inner property, this body of knowledge, opens the possibility that we could wake up from illusion and stop participating in illusion mind's vast realm of confusion and suffering.

As we gain the tools we need to develop knowledge toward a sharp and clear intellectual understanding (sems-'byung shes-rab) our ability to conduct independent inquiry grows, leading toward self-liberation. With this new tool, we can clear away confusion. We can get the right perspective on both object and subject, looking forward and backward until we can engage the emptiness of both. This emptiness, far beyond the simple nonexistence of something, is the truth of the entire field of reality and experience (sarvadharma, chos thams-cad) as Dharmadhātu.

Mind and Śūnyatā:
How Mind Manufactures

M ind proceeds by making distinctions and dividing things up. Operating with 'cause and effect' forms of cognition, it sets limits of viewing and assigns identities, each marked as exceptional. It imposes patterns and projects previous understandings. Through the dynamic that oscillates ceaselessly between one limiting view and its opposite (prapañca, spros-pa), particular perceptions arise, solidify, and proliferate, creating reality as mind knows it and makes it known.

The meanings and distinctions mind depends on are like products that mind produces, sells to itself, and then consumes. Since consuming is itself an act of producing, the process immediately starts up again. The momentum of buying, selling, and producing is unstoppable. One transaction triggers the next, and transactions build on each other, generating growing complexity. The resulting confusion only impels mind to manufacture more meanings in an effort to figure out what is going on.

These patterns and mechanisms seriously undermine our fond conviction that the mind is free. For instance, if mind operates by assigning meanings to what is experienced, and meanings depend on words and language, and language depends on already established meanings, how can mind be freed to go beyond what it already knows? The truth seems almost precisely the opposite. Caught up in an enormous array of distinctions and decisions, some made by mind itself, some passed down by society, by family, and by friends, mind is like a fly caught in a spider web. No matter how much it struggles, it finds no way out. Yet this bleak image ignores the most important point. Mind is not just the fly—it is also the spider that weaves the web. If mind could somehow recognize this, it might have a foundation for understanding that the web it weaves is śūnyatā, a mere spinning by mind that has never taken birth.

The limits that mind accepts and relies on set the terms in which we see, thoroughly conditioning the mechanism for knowing. Thus, when mind sets out to understand śūnyatā (stong-pa-nyid), it is already committed to the dualism of a subject investigating an object. But śūnyatā is *not* an object, nor is it the absence of an object. This 'not' is 'not' a 'not' that mind can work with. In mind's wish to make sense of śūnyatā, the limits of having and not-having have already come into play. We find ourselves grasping for something that cannot be grasped. Moving in the realm of 'have' and 'have not', 'exist' and 'not exist', the mind can circle endlessly within the limits of prapañca, but none of this will allow it to refine its understanding of śūnyatā. This is a serious problem, for the complete openness of śūnyatā is vital to a new understanding of mind.

Śūnyatā is often translated as 'emptiness', and if this were understood in the sense of something 'being empty', it might suggest mere negation and non-existence, categories related to dualism that mind can work with. But the 'emptiness' of śūnyatā is quite different. It is the emptiness of not having been born (nisvabhava, rang-bzhin med) or not having taken place. This emptiness gives the operations of mind no place to take hold.

Enmeshed in its web, 'fly mind' cannot understand śūnyatā. But the question remains: How is the web manufactured? What can we see about 'spider mind'? When mind draws on meanings and distinctions to point out and set identities in place, it activates a dynamic. If mind looks at the dynamic instead of its products, if it inquires into its own operations, a knowing that glimpses the web-making in process may arise.

To penetrate the meanings that mind imposes is challenging, for the patterns that mind has manufactured for so long are prefabricated, ready to be put in place almost instantaneously. To make this move—to see the mind in operation—we have to sense subtle messages that the mind is steadily sending but never explicitly pronouncing. These messages have one main theme: the insistent claim that whenever anything at all appears to mind, something else, something substantial, is operating in the background.

For instance, behind each arising thought is the message 'there is a thinker'. Can we intercept the message and see the role it plays? Can we notice the implicit claim, 'I am thinking,' or simply, 'I am'? Can we challenge the thinker's 'being there'? If so, we have come across something fundamental to mind's operations and to its (mostly unexpressed) sense of being trapped. For without the claim that something solid and real is implicit in each act of minding, there is only the minding. But minding has no substance. If only minding is going on, the freedom of śūnyatā may be accessible after all.

The thinker implicit in the thought, the triggering event inherent in the emotion, the object intrinsic to the act of perception: These are the messages that establish what is real. Each time something appears, the implicit, the intrinsic, and the inherent are already in operation, confirming that mind is trapped. But these three carriers of substance can be challenged. The mechanisms of mind are active right now, within the present moment of experience, and here and now is where we must look. In this moment, what intrinsic claims are being secretly confirmed? Is there a 'who' that is reading the message being sent? Are reactions forming? Are judgments being made? Is there 'something' to understand? Is there something to make sense of?

When we truly understand how mind operates, we no longer trust its usual ways of understanding. We are no longer in the market to buy what the mind is selling. We do not have to get stuck in what the mind affirms, and we do not have to adhere to the inherent.

But all this depends on a seeing that catches 'minding' in action, that sees the trick as it is being performed. And such a seeing depends on the light of inquiry. Revealed in this light, the implicit and intrinsic have no place to hide and so cannot play their secret role. Like a sleeper waking from a dream, we know what was unknown before: that the meanings and definitions on which the mind relies have never come to be, that even the momentum through which prapañca proliferates has never been initiated.

When the subject-object duality is transcended and śūnyatā is understood, the limits on which mind's operations depend lose their hold. In the opening lines of the Mūlamadhyamakakārikā, Nāgārjuna identifies and rejects eight fundamental limits: "no destruction/no creation; no dissolution/no eternity; no coming/no going; no difference/no sameness." ('gag-pa med-pa skye med-pa//chad-pa mcd-pa rtag med-pa//'ong-ba med-pa 'gro med-pa//tha-dad don min don-gcig min/).

Seen in the light of śūnyatā, these pairs of limiting opposites are secret sharers. Each is implicit in the other; each claims to be independent but has its foundation in the other. With no independent status, no legitimate claim to exist or not exist, they cannot bar the absolute truth (paramārthasatya, don-dam bden-pa). Cornerstones of samsara, they are nonetheless inseparable from śūnyata. When we see this to be so here and now, Nāgārjuna's string of negations becomes a celebration of freedom—the closest that words might approach to truth.

Understanding śūnyatā depends on getting to the truth of mind. The Tibetan master Vairotsana reminds us of this when he writes, "Don't analyze the words, understand the truth." In the words of a Tibetan saying: When you talk about worldly things, relevance and logic are what count, but when you talk about Dharma, the most important thing is truth.

Śūnyatā is about this truth—not truth as metaphysical abstraction or philosophical challenge, but the truth of our lives, the 'bottom line' of the mind business. Recognizing the truth of śūnyatā is the only way to let go of illusion mind, misery mind, ignorance mind, confusion mind, and intellectual mind. Nothing other than this truth can conclusively eliminate our problems, freeing us from the web of patterns and meanings that deceive us about who we are and what can be known. Only śūnyatā can deactivate the feedback loop, cut through the spider's spinning, and stop the momentum of manufacturing. Taking some therapeutical steps towards śūnyatā leads us closer and closer to the truth, whose realization is prajñā. Entering śūnyatā, mind awakens.

We understand śūnyatā by entering fully into it. But even a glimpse of understanding can be the seed from which will gradually emerge the strong stem of virtue and discipline, the healthy leaves of śamatha, vipaśyanā, and samādhi, and the beautiful flowers of the inner workings of the Bodhisattva path. As we draw closer to truth, the facets of the path begin to make sense in a comprehensive way that is intimately connected to our own life and liberation. When we explicitly recognize that our prayers, intellectual analysis, and meditation belong to the realm of mind, they can become genuine supports for the penetrating realization of śūnyatā.

At present, we may not have access to śūnyatā. But we do know how to proceed. The rTon-pa bzhi, the Four Reliances, offer precious guidance, counseling independence from the conditioning imposed by illusion mind in all its forms: "Do not rely on the personality (gang-zag) of the teacher, rely on the teachings (chos). Do not rely on the words (tshig) of the teaching, rely on the meaning (don). Do not rely on the provisional meaning (drang-don), rely on the certain meaning (nges-don). Do not rely on mind-consciousness (rnam-shes), rely on awakened wisdom (ye-shes)."

Experience of Mind:
How Mind Might Open

To engage the magic of śūnyatā, mind must transcend mind. That is the significance of the 'tā' in śūnyatā, the 'nyid' in stong-pa-nyid. This is a nuance English cannot readily capture. The 'ness' of the English 'emptiness'—even the 'ness' of that 'ness'—continues to affirm the negation-centered 'empty' that illusion mind pronounces. But 'tā' and 'nyid' engage the knowing within negation, a knowing that negates nothing at all.

For all the three yānas, understanding the relation between dngos and dngos-med, existence and non-existence, is a serious undertaking. Because the English term 'emptiness' negates, it belongs to the limiting view of non-existence that is inherently linked to existence. The emptiness of negation may serve as an intellectual step toward understanding śūnyatā, but it is not śūnyatā. The concept of 'negation' simply fails to capture the meaning.

Bound to negation, the empty or void easily becomes another entity. Pursued by conceptual mind, it can move in a nihilistic direction, turning into the rejection of all limits and structures. If we think that śūnyatā means that something that exists has to be negated or thrown away, we arrive at annihilation, a form of identity especially dangerous precisely because it claims to have recognized the mind's projects and to be free from them.

One way to counter such misunderstanding is to maintain that śūnyatā negates the reality of what is affirmed, but not its appearance. But we can also approach the issue more directly. If we do not turn śūnyatā into a conceptual problem, if we keep the focus on the immediate workings of the mind that sets up something to negate, then annihilation and negation do not arise as dangers. The more deeply and freshly we question mind's implicit claim to affirm an inherent reality intrinsic to appearance, the closer we come to understanding śūnyatā.

As engaged by the knowing of jñāna (ye-shes), śūnyatā is not any particular experience. In the dawning of 'calmness', 'awareness', 'mindfulness', 'beingness', or 'nowness', we still encounter exhibitions of the mind's minding. Mind, the charming diplomat, readily accommodates meditative experiences, just as it accommodates conceptual insights, never for a moment abandoning its claim that its mindings are real. The truth of nisvabhava goes deeper than any experience. When nothing comes into being, there can be neither manufacturer nor the process of manufacturing, neither consumer, nor consumed, nor the process of consuming.

To give us the means to transcend all stories, all claims, and all philosophizing, śūnyatā is presented in the texts in sixteen or eighteen or twenty aspects. The aim is not to arrive at some other understanding beyond interpretation. Nor is the point to strip away, cut out, isolate from, or invite some incomprehensible unknown. Instead, śūnyatā opens the mind that owns, insists, and bears witness. This means letting go of prapañca, of all limits of viewing and all exceptions adopted by mind. Opening the limited perspectives of prapañca, we arrive at the openness mind of apra-pañca—seeing everywhere at once, all encompassing, holding or possessing nothing.

The three trainings of śīla, samādhi, and prajñā cre-ate a positive momentum toward this openness. They let us contact what Dharmatā (chos-nyid) is, or let 'is' become Dharmatā. As śūnya becomes śūnyatā, the birth of Dharma wisdom shows us who we are. Recognizing self and mind, we near the starting point for the discussions of śūnyatā found in the śāstras.

Understanding śūnyatā is the key to unifying the teachings of the Dharma. The three yānas and the dif-ferent schools all have as their purpose to liberate mind, for the 84,000 teachings are the remedies for the myriad ways of fabricating karma and kleśa, and it is mind that fabricates. The five paths remove kleśa-varaṇa and jñeyavaraṇa, obscurations that mind cre-ates. In the end, all such antidotes are effective only because of śūnyatā, which makes it possible to seize the root of mind and eliminate ignorance. The Hīna-yāna severs this root, the Mahāyāna transforms it, and the Vajrayāna transcends it.

Just as śūnya (stong-pa) opens into śūnyatā (stong-pa-nyid), so to arrive at Dharma wisdom requires a transition from sems (ordinary mind) to sems-nyid. To make this journey involves something far more vast and comprehensive than 'fixing' our present circumstances or improving our lot. We begin by touching openness mind. Amazed, we may imagine this to be realization. But as our understanding matures, we recognize that we are only at a preliminary stage in approaching the development of the ten bhūmis of the Bodhisattva path, which are said in the Sūtrayāna to take thirty-two kalpas to traverse. As the heart and mind of the Bodhisattva (bodhicitta, byang-chub kyi sems) expand in compassion and deepen in wisdom, the kleśas fall apart, because they no longer have a structure within which to operate. With no place for subject and object to stand, no role for them to play, the operations of samsara give way.

For the great Bodhisattvas who advance on this path, understanding śūnyatā gives direct access to the power of mind to create, known in the ancient texts as māyā. Māyā manifests action and appearances as the expression of an untrammeled freedom. Present without ever having taken place, illusory as a mirage is illusory, māyā can manifest in all ways, for nothing can obstruct it or hold it back.

The story is told that Candrakīrti, a famed Mahāyāna master, once fed the monks of his monastery in a time of famine by milking the painting of a cow. Accepting this story as true, we ask: how could he have worked such a miracle? One answer, consistent with the understanding employed by illusion mind, might be that he had mastered the power of alchemy and could turn molecules of air to molecules of milk. But an answer more true to śūnyatā is that Candrakīrti had mastered the power of mind—the power of śūnyatā—to shape reality into any form. When the mind-imposed structure that presents 'milk' and 'painting', 'monks' and 'famine', and ultimately 'Candrakīrti' himself, has never been established, there is absolutely no need for transformation. The power of māyā is freely available.

The creations of illusion mind are grounded in the fundamental illusion of mind itself, and both are śūnyatā. A thought is born, but does not take place; a thought takes place, but has already gone. The distinctions of 'here' and 'gone', 'arising' and 'never coming to be' are all equally available, with complete flexibility. Seeing this, we see that illusion does not have to leave us deluded. Within the creative activity of mind, within thoughts, senses, energy, and identified entities, an all-illuminating light shines forth—a 'body' of mind that has no body, a kind of blessing that manifests within appearance. The eighteen śūnyatās give access to this secret body. Turning mind's power on itself, they awaken sems-nyid. And as Dignāga says, samsara and nirvana differ only in this: whether or not sems-nyid is recognized.

Two Truths of Mind:
How to Bring Freedom into View

Concepts and conceptual understanding cannot take illusion mind beyond its own illusory limits, for illusion as illusion gives conceptual mind nothing to take hold of or identify. Still, the intellect can offer bridges of inquiry that lead to śūnyatā. Toward this end, the sage Nāgārjuna, great master of the Middle Way, introduced the idea of two truths.

Conventional truth (saṁvṛtisatya, kun-rdzob bden-pa) accepts what appears to exist as real. Operating at this level, the student purifies the mind through the three trainings and practice of the six perfections, removing karma and kleśa and accumulating merit. At the level of absolute truth (paramārthasatya, don-dam bden-pa), the conventional realm has never come into being (nisvabhava, rang-bzhin med). Conception never leads to becoming pregnant, and reality does not take birth. Even not-being-born does not take birth.

Conventionally, the conventional and the absolute are separate and their two truths differ. But at the level of the absolute, the two truths are mirror images, both reflecting and embodying unity. Unborn illusion of illusion, illusion becomes the ultimate. The image in the mirror dissolves, without there having been a mirror.

Studying the interplay and significance of the two truths gives rise to understanding that supports meditation, which deepens into samādhi. The great Bodhisattvas practice this samādhi in ever more profound ways, for with no dichotomies or distinctions, there are no barriers to omniscience.

The Middle Way teachings integrate the two truths, turning the logic of illusion mind against itself. Free from both concepts and non-conceptual not-knowing, they cut through all categories and beliefs, all claims relating to 'incomprehensible' and 'inconceivable', and all nihilistic tendencies to reject the search for meaning entirely. They create an opening for Prajñā-pāramitā, for a seeing free from both 'thingness' and 'no-thingness.' The twenty-two aspects of bodhicitta, the ten stages of the path, and the five paths unfold accordingly. From the roots of samsara to enlightenment and omniscience, from the hell realms to the god realms, the continuum of the real arises as the illusory display of illusory mind.

Traditional Approaches to Mind

In order to achieve the enlightenment of the perfect Buddhas, all schools of Tibetan Buddhism study and practice the three great philosophical doctrines and meditative disciplines of Great Madhyamaka, Mahāmudrā, and Atiyoga (Tib. dBu-ma chen-po, Phyag-rgya chen-po, and rDzogs-pa chen-po). While the tradition of the Nyingma school (the Ancient

Ones) incorporates the doctrines of both Madhyamaka and Mahāmudrā, Nyingma distinguishes itself from the Sarma (gSar-ma, New) schools in that it also practices the Inner Tantras.

The four major schools of Tibetan Buddhism differ in the methodology they apply to attain mastery in meditation. The Kagyudpas, for example, may practice in accord with the preliminary practices of Mahā-mudrā (phyag-chen sngon-'gro) and the specific mind training practices that are set forth in the Six Yogas of Nāropa (rnal-'byor drug). The Sakyapas practice the teachings of path and fruition (lam-'bras) and Mantrayāna (sngags-rim). The Gelugpas base their practices on the preliminary practices (sngon-'gro) and the teachings on the stage of the path (lam-rim). The Nyingmapas practice the preliminary practices (sngon-'gro), as well as the three inner yogas of Mahā, Anu and Ati yoga.

Unless practitioners adopt the approach that relies exclusively on discipline and devotion as a basis for these practices, students in all four schools are encouraged to undertake some degree of philosophical or analytical investigation as the foundation for their training. Supported by valid intellectual understanding, a practitioner can begin to apply antidotes to see through mind's myriad faces of delusion, so that in time mind can be muted, subjugated and utterly transcended. A Tibetan saying expresses this connection: "Practicing meditation without intellectual understanding is like a person with no arms trying to climb the face of a rock."

In order to guide the student toward mastery over mind, the instructor must know the rigs-chen dgu, the nine classifications of meditative aptitude, so that he can choose the most appropriate method for transforming the particular obscurations clouding the student's mind. This approach is based on assessing the student in terms of sensory and mental elements, faculties, and mind (dhātu, khams; indriya, dbang-po; citta, sems), each of which is subdivided into three, making nine categories in all. The instructor is like a physician, judiciously prescribing the correct medicine for the particular illness that plagues the patient. The right dosage is critical as well: Too much could be deadly, while too little could be ineffective.

rDzogs-chen smin-khrid (ripening instructions) and nyan-brgyud (hearing lineage) allow the instructor to gauge the basic capacity of the student from the beginning and review signs of progress as they arise. rDzogs-chen texts and instructional guides (khrid-yigs), are not for every practitioner. They must be applied according to guidelines and a careful review of the student's experience. Once the aptitude of the student has been determined, the instructor must adhere to the guidelines of the rigs-chen dgu, the nine classifications. Just as its inner mechanism makes a clock tick in a certain way, the student's mind works in a particular set of fixed patterns that require a particular approach. By relying on the rigs-chen dgu, the instructor can closely counsel the student until he or she completely matures, and digression into wrong views or wordly samādhis is no longer a danger.

The practice tradition of Atiyoga provides another measure for how to discern the level of teaching appropriate to the ability of the student. It makes a distinction between two types of students, the snang-ba yul-gyi blo-can and rig-pa rang-snang-gi blo-can. The first must adhere to a gradual approach, while the second attains spontaneous realization. This division is comparable to another classification of meditative aptitude: the mind that develops in stages (rim-gyis-pa) and the mind that realizes at once (cig-car).

The vast majority of students have the first type of meditative aptitude, the rim-gyis-pa. While the Western intellectual is an exemplar of this kind of student, the distinguishing quality is not overt intellectualism. It is the need for contact with senses, words, and logic in order to handle and eventually transcend confusion. For this student, the instructions 'make sense' only within the boundaries of mind's domain, and he or she gradually progresses to understanding through close adherence to clear, systematic explications. Even the experiential understanding of the rim-gyis-pa is repeatedly referred back to the intellect, with its words and meanings. This literal approach makes it difficult to catch the deeper meanings of the teachings and slows progress in meditation.

At some advanced stage in this type of individual's development, his or her practice of zhi-gnas and lhag-mthong (śamatha and vipaśyanā) tends to lapse into states of bliss, clarity, and non-thought. The experience of bliss is profoundly pleasurable, and the individual may easily settle there, unable to relinquish attachment. Clarity offers vivid and transparent perception that may entrance the meditator, who feels as if she could almost count the atoms before her. And in the state of no-thought an initial sense of calm becomes so open that all thoughts, sensations and perceptions seem to vanish. This state is seemingly similar to śūnyatā, but in fact it veers toward a blankness akin to the formless realms. Whatever its attractions, in the end it is fruitless. The irony is that practitioners able to demonstrate such exceptional experiences of bliss, peace, clarity, and wakefulness may come to be seen as great meditators.

Because these meditative experiences, referred to in Tibetan as nyams, look like realization, meditators may make a 'cozy relationship' with them, but they are actually mind expressions that need to be cleared away and transformed. Deeply seductive, these nyams are obstacles to attaining the advanced meditative stages necessary to traverse the bhūmis. Mi-la-ras-pa (Milarepa) put it this way: Nyams are like clouds, while realization (rtogs) is like the pure sky.

Unless we can tell the difference between nyams and rtogs, we can be hypnotized and tricked by these experiences. Like a bee attracted to the sweetness in the center of the flower, mind hurries back again and again for the special taste of the meditative experience. But one evening, the petals may close around it, trapping the practitioner within kun-gzhi (Skt. ālaya), the all-ground consciousness.

The other type of individual, rig-pa rang-snang-gi blo-can, is very rare. An example is King Indrabodhi of Oḍḍiyāna. This exceptional type of person knows how mind can instruct mind, so that observation of experience is transmuted into realization. Experience itself becomes the natural basis for spontaneous self-liberation, without the need for a causal process. Because this clear and direct seeing is unconditioned, any minding, sensing, or perceiving is ripe for opening to awakening. Obstacles are few, and realization dawns as immediate certainty.

Such an individual readily attains spontaneous realization, free from any conceptual or temporal occupancy. The way this occurs is described by the traditional phrase "not arising; not ceasing; not arising and ceasing together." Whereas ordinary mind falsely perceives arising and ceasing, and thus reifies every instant of experience, here one naturally and effortlessly sees that when no phenomena and no single instant have ever arisen, there can equally be no ceasing or vanishing. In terms of the three times, since the mode of arising that ordinary mind takes to be the infinite 'nowness' of experience has never actually occurred, the vanishing of any phenomena or instant, perceived as the past, can also not take place. And when nothing has ever come into being or vanished, there is also no possibility for a future arising.

This profound insight radically reorients both the practitioner's understanding of reality and way of 'being' within it. Rather than viewing samsara as an insurmountable barrier to be dismantled piece by piece, the individual sees that the sword of wisdom can penetrate the veil of samsara's illusion with a single, powerful stroke. Conceptually, this realization may sound appealingly simple. But our conceptual understanding of the words used to describe the experience is categorically different from the ineffability of the experience itself, which remains beyond the reach of the intellect.

In certain exceptional cases, a student's devotion and perseverance are so profound that realization seems simple and inevitable. This was the case with Mi-la-ras-pa, who served his teacher Mar-pa with all his being, and with Kun-mkhyen 'Jigs-med Gling-pa, who was deeply devoted to Kun-mkhyen Klong-chen Rab-'byams. But such persons are rare indeed, even in a society like Tibet's, dedicated wholly to the practice of Dharma. For example, a great master of the 19th century, a gTer-ston and highly realized yogin, interviewed many meditators from 'Gu-log to lHa-sa as to the nature of their experiences. He found that those who proclaimed with confidence, "I have realized rig-pa," could rarely distinguish rig-pa (vidyā) from kun-gzhi rnam-shes (ālayavijñāna).

Given the many obstacles that can arise, it is critical that both student and teacher be realistic and honest with themselves and each other from the outset. If the student has a limited accumulation of merit, or has received only a few, disparate instructions on meditation, or reads and studies meditation guidebooks from various traditions, he or she will lack the stable foundation for cultivating meditative experience in accord with the approaches of Madhyamaka, Mahāmudrā, or Atiyoga. When their meditation does not conform to the signs and indications clearly explained in the texts, students may well become disheartened and confused; in the end they may even fall into despair. Alternatively, they may mistake peak meditative experiences or worldly samādhis for true realization, developing a false sense of confidence that undermines all chance for true achievement.

Ground, path, and fruition as outlined in the Vajrayāna are much higher than the worldly absorptions of advanced meditative states. Seeing the absorptions as a valid method to advance along the path to liberation is a fundamental error. While it may be easy from a outsider's perspective to dismiss this danger as self-evident, meditators should make every effort to truly acknowledge it from the beginning. Otherwise this very obstacle may arise.

The way to prevent these confusions is through sustained practice and good counsel. If a student finds and stays with a qualified master, meditating at some length daily for at least a year and a half, with periodic review of meditative experiences with the master, meditation can be supremely beneficial, truly a lamp illuminating the path to enlightenment.

A skilled instructor will also know the various ways to view and relate the different Dharma teachings in terms of rim-gyis-pa and cig-car-ba, gradual and sudden. For example, the Vaibhāṣika approach is more gradual than Sautrāntika, and both are more gradual than Mādhyamika. Svātantrika Mādhyamika is more gradual than Prāsaṅgika, and Sūtrayāna more gradual than Mantrayāna. Outer Tantras are more gradual than Inner Tantras, Mahāyoga is more gradual than Atiyoga, and in Atiyoga the Sems-sde and Klong-sde are more gradual than Man-ngag gi sde.

Two texts that offer guidance for both teacher and student on these vital points are the Gol-shor-tsar-gcod-seng-ge-nga-ro of Kun-mkhyen 'Jigs-med Gling-pa, and the Phyag-chen-khrid-yig of Dwags-po bKra-shis rNam-rgyal. In addition, A-'dzom 'Brug-pa's Khyad-par-gyi-khrid-yig delineates four stages of practice (rnal-'byor bzhi-rim) and expresses in a pithy and cogent manner how practice can deviate into bliss, clarity and no-thought, a direct cause for rebirth in the god realms, and thus an obstacle on the path.

Evaluating Understanding of Mind

Regardless of differences in presentation among the three great systems of dBu-ma chen-po, Phyag-rgya chen-po, and rDzogs-pa chen-po, they each transmit explicit guidelines for verifying progress on the path and clearly enumerate the methods for exhausting both emotional and cognitive obscurations. For example, in the Prasannapadā, an important commentary on Nāgārjuna's Mūlamadhyamakakārikā, Candrakīrti explains twenty-two kinds of bodhicitta (sems-bskyed), the ten bhūmis (sa bcu), and the five paths (lam lnga). Following such approaches, it eventually becomes possible to make the important distinctions between sems and rig-pa (citta and vidyā), kun-gzhi and chos-sku (ālaya and Dharmakāya), and rnam-shes and ye-shes (vijñāna and jñāna).

Both student and teacher can gain much clarity by becoming familiar with the outlines of the path found in different traditions, together with the central Mādhyamika paradigm of the stages of practices. Masters of the Mādhyamika tradition identify four advanced meditative stages: emptiness (bden-med), unity (zung-'jug), aprapañca (spros-bral), and equality (mnyam-nyid). Alternatively, in sGam-po-pa's Four Stages of Yoga (rnal-'byor bzhi-rim), the four highest stages of meditation are outlined following the teachings of Maitripa: one-pointedness (rtse-gcig), aprapañca (spros-bral), one taste (ro-gcig), and non-meditation sgom-med/. Each of these stages has three divisions (che-'bring-chung-gsum). The rDzogs-chen tradition also speaks of four stages, known as the sNang-ba bzhi.

All of the various presentations of the stages of meditation can be simplified into a twofold division universally accepted by the three vehicles as well as the four schools of Tibetan Buddhism: the occasion of meditative equipoise (mnyam-bzhag) and the occasion of ensuing attainment (rjes-thob). Each of these is described in different ways by various schools, but both Sūtrayāna and Mantrayāna present a threefold classification of meditation as experienced by

Bodhisattvas in terms of these two occasions. The three samādhis are the samadhi of the view of illusion (sgyu-ma'i lta-ba'i ting-nge-'dzin), the samādhi of the indestructible diamond view (rdo-rje lta-ba'i ting-nge-'dzin), and the samādhi of heroic traversing (dpa'-bar 'gro-ba'i ting-nge-'dzin). The first samādhi is related to the ensuing attainment (rjes-thob) experienced by the Bodhisattva following meditation. The second samādhi is the mnyam-bzhag, the meditative equipoise of Bodhisattvas on the higher bhūmis, or stages of the Bodhisattva path. The third samādhi leads the Bodhisattva through the bhūmis to the attainment of complete enlightenment.

In this progression, the crucial transition is the shift from sems to sems-nyid, the full understanding of the mind as śūnyatā, whether the realization of sems-nyid arises with the fourth initiation of the Vajrayāna or through the meditations of the Great Vehicle. According to Mahāmudrā (Phyag-rgya Chen-po) and Atiyoga (rDzogs-pa Chen-po), sems-nyid is what the "pointing out instructions" point out (sems-nyid ngo-'phrod). If the realization of sems-nyid (sems-nyid rtogs-pa) of the Mantrayāna is the same as the stong-pa-nyid mngon-sum du rtogs-pa of the Sūtrayāna, then in terms of the five-path structure described in the Sūtras and śāstras, sems-nyid arises as the practitioner enters the Path of Seeing (mthong-lam).

This direct seeing (mngon-sum du mthong), refined through cultivation of the eighteen kinds of śūnyatā and delineated and celebrated in the teachings of the

Prajñāpāramitā and the Madhyamaka śāstras, marks the first bhūmi, or stage, of the Bodhisattva Path. As the limits of prapañca lose their hold (spros-pa'i mtha' thams-cad dang bral-ba), all conventional meanings and perceptions are transcended (sgro-'dogs thams-cad dang bral-ba).

According to the Abhisamayālaṁkāra, the Sūtrā-laṁkāra, and the Prasannapadā, upon reaching the first bhūmi, the Bodhisattva manifests 1,200 beautiful qualities. If practitioners who gain understanding of śūnyatā do not show these qualities, does that indicate their understanding is incomplete or erroneous? There are different views on this question. Sa-skya Paṇḍita recommends that we follow the guidance of the Sūtras in authenticating attainment, while other commentators say that these qualities characterize the practitioner's meditation, so that no one but the practitioner would know. Some say that the qualities are hidden and appear in the bardo after the physical body has been relinquished, like a new-born garuḍa who soars into flight as soon as the shell of its egg is broken, or like the light from a lantern concealed in a vase that shines forth when the vase is broken open. To this interpretation, Sa-skya Paṇḍita replies tongue-in-cheek that if holding on to the physical body is the only obstacle, the solution would be easy, yet yogins do not choose it!

Lama Mi-pham offers a valuable insight into this question when he explains that the reason the qualities may not manifest is that realization is not yet the actual understanding of śūnyatā (don-gyi ye-shes), but rather the clarity of śūnyatā (dpe-yi ye-shes). It is like the new moon compared to the full moon, or like a reflection of the moon. Over time, the realization of dpe-yi ye-shes shines forth, grows, and develops to completion (gsal-rgyas-rdzogs). At this point don-gyi ye-shes emerges and the first bhūmi is attained. Only then do the great qualities of the Bodhisattva appear. When Nāropa received pointing out instructions from Tilopa, this may have been an instance of direct attainment of the first bhūmi and don-gyi ye-shes). In general, however, the introduction to sems-nyid will lead to dpe-yi ye-shes, which, like the waxing moon, increases in depth, clarity, and stability, leading to don-gyi ye-shes.

In terms of the traditional path structure, I believe that dpe-yi ye-shes arises at the end of the second path, known as the path of linking (sbyor-lam). The sbyor-lam includes four levels, known as heat (drod-pa), summit (rtse-mo), acceptance (bzod-pa), and highest worldly dharma (chos-mchog). It is at the completion of the fourth level, sbyor-lam chos-mchog, that the light of śūnyatā begins to dawn (gsal-snang). One could say that understanding has been growing slowly, starting on the path of accumulation and continuing through the path of linking. Or one could say that the sun of realization that will rise on the path of seeing begins to dawn at the end of the path of linking. In either case, only as this light truly emerges does the transition to the first bhūmi take place, allowing the qualities of the Bodhisattvas to manifest.

Nonetheless, dpe-yi ye-shes is direct seeing. Direct seeing is unmediated (mngon-sum-du) while inference (rjes-su dpag-pa) is indirect, requiring a means, a reason, or evidence. dPe-yi ye-shes realization of emptiness is direct, but direct in the manner of inference (mngon-sum rjes-su dpag-pa'i tshul-du rtogs-pa) for understanding comes through the blessings of the lama or through an image (stong-nyid don-spyi) such as 'like the sky' or 'beyond mind'.

Masters of dBu-ma chen-po, Phyag-rgya chen-po, and rDzogs-pa chen-po have composed numerous commentaries on just these crucial points. Here we are just making a few connections without trying to be systematic, in order to give a sense of what is at stake. Mantrayāna practitioners should think these questions through carefully. Even for new Dharma students such reflection is valuable, for understanding the context in which different practices are undertaken clarifies how the path works. Knowledge of the structure of the path is precious and powerful protection, for it puts personal practice in the proper perspective and builds confidence in the process of transformation.

Pointing out Mind:
How to Protect Understanding

Some Western students are strongly drawn to the aspect of the Mantrayāna in which the teacher 'points out' (ngo-'phrod) the nature of mind to the student. They may believe that it offers a more direct path to realization than the cultivation of śīla, samādhi, and prajñā. If students understand this approach superficially or out of context, however, they may end up with a perspective that is too simplistic, one that does not fully allow for the delusive nature of mind.

The Sūtras say, "Not a single Buddha sees, has seen, or will see mind." If the Buddhas do not see the mind, how can it be pointed out? This is not a question to be waved off as a charming paradox. It has real, practical significance. When the student goes to the teacher for teachings that point out the nature of mind, a complex structure has been presupposed. Someone does the pointing, someone hopes to understand, and there is something to be pointed out. Illusion mind has set up this structure, and the fact that we accept it means that illusion mind is in firm control. When we start meditation on this basis, we 'see' the mind only through interpretations made by the mind we want to see. Indeed, as long as we are ordinary individuals of the rim-gyis-pa type, what other choice do we have?

The sacred instructions found in dBu-ma Chen-po, Phyag-rgya Chen-po, and rDzogs-pa Chen-po certainly have the power to produce realization. So whether the student 'gets it' or not will depend on whether the instructions are being properly tailored to the student, according to the rig-chen-dgu, and on whether the student is being properly prepared. For all but the greatest yogins, such as Saraha, Tilopa, Virūpa, or Padmasambhava, thorough preparation, consisting of accumulating merit and exhausting some measure of karma and kleśa, is essential, for otherwise the mind that meditates on mind or sets out to 'see' mind will be illusion mind. Illusion mind cannot see sems-nyid, any more than a camera with the shutter closed can take a picture. Illusion mind's meditation may produce inner calm, greater clarity, and joy, but it cannot produce penetrating insight into mind and reality. Only when the three trainings lighten the burden of karma and kleśa is sems-nyid accessible. And it is the seeing of sems-nyid that opens the 'seeingless-ness' of śūnyatā.

Even when the teacher who 'points out' mind points out that there is no mind to point out, will the student have any way to understand what is being said? Without insight into how illusion mind sets up and is set up, the student will remain caught in the framework of 'subject-object-instructions-something to do'. It is not enough to look at ordinary mind with ordinary mind and say, "There is nothing here." Such negation is based on a mind made up in advance, and 'made-up mind' can easily turn 'no mind' into another manifestation of illusion mind. One must know who is saying "no mind," or 'no mind' will just be the imaginary object of a deluded subject. Nor do 'there' and 'here' apply, for realization is not limited by ordinary space and time. Following the words 'mind' and 'no-mind', we are in the language realm where objects have or not-have qualities, and we have missed the point again. As Śāntideva reminds us: "Absolute realization is not the realm of mind." (don-dam blo-yi spyod-yul min). But what choice do we have? Without words, how can the ordinary, rim-gyis-pa individual understand?

If a student who has received pointing-out instructions is confident he or she can distinguish rig-pa from kun-gzhi rnam-shes, this is a great accomplishment. But where total confidence is lacking, it is good to question further, to be sure that time is not being wasted. Questioning at this level—questioning our own understanding—does not come easily. If we are following what we believe are the instructions of the teacher; if we see what we think we are supposed to see, according to what we think is being pointed to, why should we question? Yet if results do not show up over time, in the form of increasing compassion, less susceptibility to karma and kleśa, and deepening faith in the Triple Gem; if we are not making progress and the jaundice of illusion mind is not cured, we may begin to wonder if we have missed the point. What is the problem? It may not be a failure of the Dharma or the teacher; it may be that we have not understood correctly.

A Few Key Distinctions and Questions

Wisdom is not wondering mind or wandering mind.

Śūnyatā cannot possibly be single negation.

Perception is not non-dual awareness.

A focused not-knowing cannot develop śamatha.

Stubbornly holding imagination is not visualization.

Dullness and 'lostness' cannot transform samsaric mind.

Collapsing perception is not the gateway to samādhi.

Losing yourself in the senses is not selflessness awakening.

Glorified mind has nothing whatsoever to do with realization.

Hanging on to mind games is not the continuity of meditation.

Watching the watcher is just endlessly chasing your tail.

Pointing out is not looking 'according to'.

How can we reconcile the dichotomy of mind and its manifestations through meditation?

How can subject and object become 'oneness experience', so we do not hang on to time?

Can we let the unborn features of subject and object neither come nor go, so that only being remains?

The wish for understanding exerts enormous pressure on ordinary mind, for not-understanding has no meaning, offers nothing to relate to, supports no sense of identity, and is not fulfilling. But to understand at the level of what has meaning for mind is to uphold the conventions of conventional reality, to play along with the rules of the game. Only transcending the limits of prapañca could end the game, but this is something ordinary mind cannot afford to do. Instead, it turns 'transcend' into another limit, or makes 'no-mind' into the opposite of 'mind'. Safely established within the realm of illusion mind, the meditator accepts the regime of meditation and holds fast to the specific position called 'understanding' or 'not-understanding'.

The nature of the negation resulting from an analytical understanding of not-self or from the pointing-out instructions of 'empty mind' is especially difficult to recognize'. This negation may present itself as the result of successful practice while remaining inference. Mind holds on to the 'not', insisting on a private, special territory. The meditator may end up clinging to a subtle self, akin to the pudgala-atma of the tirthika's shes-rig-gi-skye-bo. 'Jam-dbyangs mKhyen-brtse dBang-po says: "Do not be tainted by objects to be grasped and do not be contaminated by the grasping mind." (gzung-ba'i yul-gyis ma-gos-pa/'dzin-pa sems-kyis ma-bslad-pa/) Or, as Mañjughoṣa taught Lama Sa-skya Chen-po: "If there is any subtle grasping, that is not the view (lta-ba)."

Such possibilities of confusion and self-deception occur in any kind of serious meditation practice, whether it follows the Mantrayāna pointing-out instructions or the Prajñāpāramitā. Everyone gets stuck with meaning problems, no-meaning problems, negation problems, assertion problems. The rim-gyis-pa mind can spin around a long time, puzzling out the patterns and fitting the pieces together.

If we have not first thoroughly investigated how illusion mind operates, a penetrating meditative experience in itself will not necessarily protect us from such difficulties. The memory of "once upon a time I glimpsed" does not have the power to remove not-knowing, karma, and kleśa. Beautiful experiences or flashing ideas, even moments of rare insight, are not enough to penetrate the not-knowing that preoccupies the mind at a deep level.

Not-knowing's insistent momentum moves rapidly back and forth from subject to object. The shifts are subtle, and the points of transition are covered over, but their cumulative effect is to drain away the vitality of intelligence. Beneath the surface of perception a vague, repetitive cycle shimmers, an elusive rhythm, like the tick-tock of a giant clock, hypnotizing and dulling the mind without ever clearly manifesting particular thoughts or perceptions. When the momentum grows strong enough, we sink into a lost, fuzzy state, known in Tibetan as bying-ba, which we may mistake for the calm of zhi-gnas (śamatha). As we subtly identify with this hypnotized feeling, this confused dullness, it becomes our nest, whether we find it comfortable or not. Alternatively, not-knowing may manifest in a kind of excitement (rgod-pa) that mimics the quality of being awake. Strong, clear thoughts pop up repeatedly, fascinating us. Though we may feel full of energy, mind is out of control, concentration is interrupted, and inner wholeness is lost.

Since the karmic power of not-knowing has an almost inconceivable momentum, we need to consistently renew intelligence to see how illusion recurs. Such insight is necessary not just in our meditation practice, but in the immediate situations of daily life, for wherever we are, mind is with us always. To investigate the innermost mechanisms of mind in this ongoing way 'points out' the entire domain of Dharma. Practitioners can apply it as a highly effective tool, no matter what their stage or method of practice.

While Tibetan schools give varying emphasis to analytic meditation (dpyad-sgom) and resting meditation ('jog-sgom), both are useful and important. Practicing the pointing-out instructions belongs to 'jog-sgom. Like all practices, it runs the risk that errors will go unrecognized unless a skilled teacher is available to offer guidance by means of examination and review at each step. Combining 'jog-sgom with dpyad-sgom gives a basic method for testing, refining, and protecting the understanding that comes from 'jog-sgom.

It will be beneficial if students embarking on the path of the Dharma undertake serious and sustained analysis of the suffering and confusion caused by the tyranny of mind, for the understanding that results can be self-liberating. So powerful is the truth of insight into mind that we may even be able to halt or reverse the momentum that drives samsara. If we can discover this secret hidden within our intrinsic knowing, we may also find within a vast treasury of other wish-fulfilling jewels.

Freedom of Mind:
How to Heal Dichotomies

At each stage of Dharma study and practice, it is vital for practitioners to see the mechanisms of mind's endless spinning and to identify its dialogues, feedback, and read-outs. We are all magical weavers at the spinning wheel we call samsara, perpetuating a seamless continuity of illusion and delusion. But if we put the wheel in 'rewind mode', investigating carefully, we may begin to realize how cycle after cycle, life after life, permutation after permutation, this spinning momentum has been the one constant, the fundamental principle driving our being.

Just as we cannot perceive the movement of our planet earth with our senses, so we cannot ordinarily perceive this driving force—not the endless transmigration through the realms at the macro level, nor the uninterrupted agitation of our minds at the micro level. It is only when we find some stasis, some experience of stationary rest, that we can possibly begin to see how terribly, mind-numbingly dizzying our experience has been.

As the tell-tale mark of our existence, this seemingly unending activity extends out in all directions and in every expression of being. It captures not only the individual psyche, but the collective drama of the entire cosmos. Individuals, families, associations, nations, cultures and civilizations are all sustained by the ever present, inexhaustible spinning of mind itself. Spinning sentient minds collide and conjoin, orbiting in ever more and larger conglomerations. There seems no end to the actors and roles their force can create, from the most helpless, pitiable human being to the most powerful and arrogant nation.

This regime of movement without awareness, movement away from awareness, sustains our reality. If we trace it back, we come to realize how its infinite manifestations have conspired to keep us oblivious to our real condition. Once we step back, we realize where we have been since beginningless time, where we are, and where we are inevitably headed.

It can take a long time to understand the magic of mind. Like the most territorial of animals, as soon as mind grasps, it stakes a claim, builds a nest, and makes babies. One perception seeds three, four, and five subsequent perceptions, and soon awareness is lost. Dreams mix with memories, emotions mix with basic confusion. In the shimmering, rippling surface of appearance, one story leads compulsively to the next, making the action-reaction momentum unstoppable.

Bonded to this flickering, spinning light show, awareness staggers on, always on the verge of exhaustion. No freshness, no deep, settled resting can occur. Until our own analytic and meditative research shows us clearly and with certainty how any business mind undertakes thrusts us into this hopeless realm of ignorance, karma, and kleśa, our failure to understand the mechanism of minding prevents us from releasing ourselves into being.

As long as we cannot distinguish being from mind, meaning from language, and sensing from perception, we are trapped in confusion and vulnerable to suffering. But when our understanding finally begins to penetrate mind's maneuvers, we have a chance not to engage, not to chase, not to manipulate. We can simply open to the facticity of what is so. Protected and uplifted by right seeing, no longer led in circles by the mind, we have the chance to be independent and free.

As we refine the accurate seeing that understands the delusiveness of 'mind business', a gradual process of healing can commence. The endless spinning of subject and object can be relaxed, bringing us closer and closer to direct experience. Knowing that internal dialogues lead nowhere, we slow down, and mind stops chasing its own tail. Calm at last, mind wakes up naturally, and can more readily establish itself in a meditative mode that moves toward śūnyatā. Less entangled in dichotomy, mind grows whole and simple in a deeply meaningful way that words cannot capture.

When the mind's spinning relaxes, perception can begin to open up. Ordinary perception, shaped by the spinning mechanisms of mind, makes it its ongoing project to maintain the separation of subject and object. In this way of perceiving, the subject grasps the object, recognizes it, identifies how it fits with the subject's territory, and then reacts to it with either attraction or repulsion to expand or protect that territory. The senses must 'make sense'. Experience must be 'figured out' to make it match certain preexisting patterns. This requires endless, exhausting, continuous interpretation, an obligation we take on in order to earn recognition as rational, reasonable beings.

The senses, however, have the capacity to operate in ways other than grasping, labeling, and reacting, ways that are less destructive, interruptive, and confusing and more cooperative. When the constant spinning relaxes, sensing can open up into a dance of being in the world, an incisive demonstration of beauty and love, a refreshing flow of peacefulness. The stream of experience can heal the fragmentation of consciousness. Our being is filled with a contentment that promotes stability, and we do not spin out of control at the slightest provocation. Closer to the flow of time, no longer out of presence, we are not attracted to daydreams or fantasies. We do not waste time on dramas and dialogues, for the nectar of meaningfulness provides the nourishment we seek. Each moment becomes precious, a wellspring of great joy and deep pleasure.

When the distractions of confused mind-spinning no longer steal our time and the suffering inherent in samsara-spinning no longer distresses our spirit, we find new resources for accomplishment. Such freedom is reliable in a way the old mind-business is not, for knowledge of how mind works is a genuine refuge. It leads us into wholeness, love, compassion, and joy, into seeinglessness that embodies śūnya and stabilizes as śūnyatā.

How to Step onto the Path

Students who wish to develop confidence in the Dharma based on genuine knowledge can become familiar with the stages of the path, study the great accomplishments of the masters of the past, and apply the three trainings to their own lives, observing the results for themselves. Studying the qualities of the Three Jewels—Buddha, Dharma, and Sangha—and comparing them to the qualities of samsaric illusion mind with its governing principles of karma, kleśa, and ignorance, the individual can see what is reliable. The beauty of mkhyen-brtse-nus-pa, the enlightened knowledge, love, and power manifested by the holders of the lineage of realization, uplifts and inspires, like daylight suddenly visible at the end of a treacherous tunnel. Here the weary heart and mind can find shelter and guidance. Gradually they can accumulate the resources they need to get clear of the trickery of illusion mind.

Traditional texts give eight qualities of the Sangha, summarized in terms of knowledge and liberation (rig-pa dang grol-ba); eight qualities of the Dharma, summarized as four relating to the truth of cessation and four on the truth of the path; and innumerable special qualities of the Buddha, sometimes summarized as the twenty-one qualities of the Dharmakāya. As we learn about these qualities and how they are developed along the path of awakening, the descriptions gradually cease being empty words. Growing appreciation for the Three Jewels brings about a different orientation toward our own life. If these heights of wisdom and compassion are also treasures hidden within each human life, what could be more worthwhile than stepping onto this path? What could bring more meaning to our lives than surrendering to the transforming power of enlightenment?

The natural outcome of such practice is taking refuge. In time, taking refuge leads to the rising of bodhicitta (sems-bskyed), the mind set on enlightenment for the sake of all beings. Three ways of developing bodhicitta are described: the way of the shepherd who guides the sheep to safety, following after them; the way of the boatman, who rides along with the passengers he conducts; and the way of the king, who first secures his own power and freedom so that he is able to rescue others. These three approaches belong to what is called conventional bodhicitta, the intention or wish to reach enlightenment for the sake of all beings, prepared for with instruction from a master and formalized with the taking of the Bodhisattva vow. Conventional bodhicitta ripens into ultimate bodhicitta, which emerges on the approach to the first bhūmi. Compassion joins with wisdom, and the wish to dedicate oneself to the benefit of all beings becomes a working truth. No longer conceptualized in terms of self and other, bodhicitta flows naturally.

A good way of organizing practice, whether we focus on intellectual analysis, meditation and prayer, devotion, or work for the welfare of others, is the Three Excellences or Three Treasures (dam-pa gsum). According to dPal-sprul Rinpoche, we start by generating bodhicitta (sbyor-ba sems-bskyed) as the basic motivation for any action. The more we expand our focus to envision the benefit of numberless beings, the more pure our intention becomes. This is the first treasure. The second treasure is the main practice (dngos-gzhi), whatever it may be. It is undertaken whole-heartedly, without emotional reactivity or negativity. The more we engage this activity contemplatively, the more the benefits for ourselves and others.

The third treasure is the dedication of the merit produced (bsngo-ba) to the enlightenment of all beings. Dedicated in accord with the immeasurable purposes of the Bodhisattva lineage, before the positive momentum of the main practice can be interrupted by emotionality, merit is like a drop of water that merges into the depths of the boundless ocean. It endures until the practitioner is enlightened, creating an increasingly stronger link to the lineage of realization, so that the power of compassion grows and matures. The accumulation of merit (puṇyasambhara, bsod-nams kyi tshogs) thus ripens into the great love of the Buddhas and Bodhisattvas, while the accumulation of the wisdom of śūnyatā (jñeyasambhara, ye-shes kyi tshogs) ripens into their great knowledge.

As we understand more deeply the way mind operates, we grow in wisdom, which in turn transforms our understanding and practice of devotion and compassion. Letting go of mind projections, relaxing the underlying grasping, confusion, and fear that characterize ordinary action—even acts of devotion—heart and mind simply open to the all-pervading blessings of the Dharmadhātu. Free of mind's demanding structure, our prayers become transparent, and this makes them far more effective.

Today there is so little time for meditation and so much agitation 'in the air' that simply developing peace of mind, inner honesty, and self-trust becomes a big task. Any progress we can make in this direction is important, for it helps us know what we are doing in the most fundamental way. If we begin with mindfulness and move beyond just watching, we come in contact with awareness beyond doer and watcher. This awareness is flexible and penetrating, uplifting and protecting. It leads invariably in wholesome directions. As we stop spinning the web of mind, we can protect intelligence and energy from loss and discover mind's magical operations.

Knowledge of mind makes it possible to treat mind more cooperatively, bringing out accomplishment, appreciation, and understanding, the hallmark of genuine spiritual progress. Sharing goodness with all around us, we find life rich and fulfilling. In touch with our being, everything we experience or do becomes meaningful, no matter where we are or who we are with. My wish for each of you reading this book is that this becomes the truth of your life.

PART TWO

The Challenge of
Studying Dharma Today

Dharma Study in Tibet

The course of study that supports the three trainings has been worked out over the course of two millennia. In Tibet, all schools take as the foundation for study the Sūtras and śāstras. Vinaya, Abhidharma, and Prajñāpāramitā are considered the three most fundamental subjects. They are supplemented with training in the Middle Way teachings (Madhyamaka, dBu-ma) and the study of logic and epistemology (Pramāṇa, Tshad-ma), two strands of śāstra teachings cultivated to develop clarity and specificity and to uphold the Dharma in debate. Five supplemental fields of study are also pursued for their practical benefit: language, medicine, art and architecture, social sciences, and history. A preliminary course of study in all these topics requires a minimum of five years. More commonly, ten years or more is necessary.

In the Nyingma tradition, study might begin with the Jātakas and Avadānas, stories of the Buddha and his disciples in past lives that teach action in accord with the Dharma. Also important are texts that introduce blo-sbyong (mind training); the Bodhicaryā-vatāra of Śāntideva (a comprehensive guide to the Bodhisattva path, most often studied together with

commentaries by Kun-bzang dPal-ldan and dPal-
sprul Rin-po-che); and the Kun-bzang Bla-ma'i Zhal-
lung of dPal-sprul Rinpoche.

Study of the five major subjects is organized
around thirteen principal śāstras identified by the nine-
teenth-century master gZhan-dga', as well as other
key texts. For the Vinaya, students would rely as well
on Lo-chen Dharmaśrī's commentary on the sDom-
gsum rNam-nges, a text by mNga'-ris Paṇ-chen that
sets forth the training to be followed by monks, Bodhisattvas, and followers of the Mantrayāna. For Madhyamaka studies, students might focus on Āryadeva's
Catuḥśataka, Śāntarakṣita's Madhyamakālaṁkāra, and
Candrakīrti's Madhyamakāvatāra, followed by the
Mūlamadhyamakakārikā of Nāgārjuna.

To explore the philosophical tradition more com-
prehensively, students would study the works of
Bhāvaviveka, Haribhadra, and other later masters of
the Mādhyamika school, as well as Maitreya's Abhisamayālaṁkāra, an invaluable guide for the systematic
study of Prajñāpāramitā. Other comprehensive philosophical texts relied on by Nyingma students are Lama
Mi-pham's mKhas-'jug, the Shes-bya Kun-khyab of
Kong-sprul Blo-gros mTha'-yas, and Kun-mkhyen
Klong-chen-pa's Ngal-gso sKor-gsum.

Students who entered into the Sūtrayāna teachings
more fully would study all four major schools of philosophy—Vaibhāṣika, Sautrāntika, Cittamātra, and
Mādhyamika—analyzing the nature of mind and experience from the perspective of each. The Vaibhāṣika and

Sautrāntika frame their analysis in terms related to the Abhidharma. The Cittamātra (Mind Only) school, which asserts the supremacy of mind, did not flourish in Tibet, but great paṇḍitas integrated its insights with those of the Mādhyamika.

Mādhyamika, based on the works of Nāgārjuna, is considered by followers of the Mahāyāna to be the highest philosophical school. It was developed to clarify the Mahāyāna view and path, to uphold the Mahāyāna in dialogue with those who focused exclusively on uprooting the kleśas, and to defend the Buddhist view in exchanges with outsiders. Mādhyamika analyzes the depth of mind, showing that through sustained inquiry the mind that inquires can become wisdom, inseparable from Dharmadhātu.

The other schools of Tibetan Buddhism also rely on the Jātakas and Avadānas, blo-sbyong texts, and the Bodhicaryāvatāra, and study the five major subjects. The Kagyudpa tend to focus chiefly on practice. In their study of the śāstras, they give special importance to the rGyud Bla-ma (Uttaratantra) of Maitreya and its commentary by 'Jam-mgon Kong-sprul, and to the thirteen śāstras designated by gZhan-dga'. The Gelugpa and the Sakyapa both generally emphasize intellectual training at the outset, starting with logic and epistemology. The Gelugpa rely on two fundamental texts of Tsong-kha-pa, the Lam-rim Chen-mo and the sNgags-rim Chen-mo. The Sakyapa traditionally focused on eighteen śāstras, but in more recent times have studied the thirteen śāstras emphasized by gZhan-dga' and his commentaries on each, which summarize the commentaries of the Indian masters. They also rely on the Lam-'bras of Sa-skya Kun-dga' sNying-po.

These are only broad descriptions, for there are hundreds and thousands of Sūtras, Tantras, and commentaries, and their study can proceed in many different ways. The renowned master Kaḥ-thog Situ prepared a syllabus based on a hundred key texts, many of which are now lost, but few individuals can study in such depth. More recently new curriculums have been instituted in light of changed conditions, such as the curriculum I worked on in 1967 with two colleagues from the Gelugpa and Sakyapa schools for the newly founded Central Institute of Higher Tibetan Studies in Sarnath, India.

In Tibet, inquiry into the workings of mind depended on Mantrayāna as well as Sūtrayāna. Here the major schools rely on different texts and approaches. The Sakyapa turn to the rGyud-sde spyi'i rnam-bzhag, the lJon-shing chen-mo-khrid, and the rTsa-rgyud rtag pa gnyis pa. The Kagyupa also rely on the rTsa-rgyud rtag-pa gnyis-pa, as well as the Zab-mo nang-don of Rang-byung rDo-rje. The Gelugpa follow the gSang-'dus, the bDe-mchog, and the 'Jigs-'byed Tantras.

In the Nyingma tradition, study that is grounded in Mantrayāna would begin with the general and special preliminary practices and works and would include the following teachings:

bKa'-ma: The bKa'-ma teachings of the Outer Tantras (Kriyā, Caryā and Yoga) and Inner Tantras (Mahā, Anu, and Atiyoga). The Inner Tantras are collected in the rNying-ma'i rGyud-'bum, said to have included originally 100,000 texts. First assembled by Ratna Gling-pa, the rGyud-'bum was later edited by Kun-mkhyen 'Jigs-med Gling-pa and also by dGe-rtse Mahāpaṇḍita ('Gyur-med Tshe-dbang mChog-grub), each of whom composed a catalogue of the texts. An authoritative edition was printed at sDe-dge monastery. Hundreds of bKa'-ma commentaries were written by Buddhaguhya, Vimalamitra, and other great masters: four hundred authors in all.

gTer-ma: Texts concealed for later recovery by disciples of Padmasambhava reborn for that very purpose. Since many gTer-ma present the threefold structure of ground, path, and fruit, the total number of teachings is extremely vast. There have been some 1,200 gTer-ma masters in all. Many key texts are collected in more than sixty volumes of the Rin-chen gTer-mdzod, while additional gTer-ma are preserved in the collected works of the gTer-stons.

With so many gTer-ma, monasteries specialize in certain sādhanas, or in the cycle of teachings associated with a particular master, such as the Northern Treasures revealed by Rig-'dzin rGod-ldem or the Bla-ma dGongs-pa 'Dus-pa of Sangs rgyas Gling-pa. The six major Nyingma monasteries, as well as their hundreds of branch monasteries, all maintained their own sādhanas, each having both an explanation lineage and hearing lineage.

Collected Writings: Many Nyingma masters wrote fifteen volumes or more. Some texts related to the bKa'-ma teachings, others to topics ranging across all fields of knowledge, from healing, philosophy, and meditation to astrology, special powers, and experience in the bardo.

Ritual: Training in practices such as chanting, sacred music and dance, mandala creation, prayer, visualization, offering gtor-ma, ritual order, and robes. Training for even a single Tantra could be very complex, requiring several months to complete.

Art: Creation and empowering of art, including symbols of the five aspects of the Enlightened Ones: sku, gsung, thugs, yon-tan, and phrin-las (Body, Speech, Mind, Qualities, and Action).

Upholding the Teachings
in a Changing World

The Dharma in Tibet offered inconceivable riches. At the time of the first transmission, great masters such as Padmasambhava, Vimalamitra, and Śānta-rakṣita initiated Tibetans into the whole range of teachings and practices. Later, great monasteries and thousands of smaller centers passed on a wealth of different traditions. Eight major transmission lineages evolved that were later organized into four schools. Each lineage has its own traditions, texts, and lineage holders, but some are now only rarely encountered.

To master even one aspect of these teachings requires enormous time, effort, and energy, as well as contact with lamas who hold the transmission lineages. Only the greatest masters, such as 'Jam-dbyangs mKhyen-brtse dBang-po and 'Jam-mgon Kong-sprul, can engage the whole field of knowledge. Most lamas develop a few areas of expertise, such as mantra and prayer, ritual practice, or extended meditative retreats. Some may hold the blessing lineages for numerous texts without having received the explanation lineage or studied the teachings; others may emphasize philosophical study or study of Vinaya. Some abandon the eight worldly dharmas, taking

leave of all mundane concerns; others develop admin-
istrative skills or exercise leadership within the
Sangha. Still others become oracles, physicians,
astrologers, artists, or dancers.

In the past, these different threads of Tibetan
Buddhism were woven into a seamless whole within
the great monasteries, where monks could join their
efforts and knowledge. Today monasteries in exile
lack the resources to function in this way, and students may be cut off from many aspects of the tradition. A young mkhan-po sent off after only eight to ten
years of study to teach at another institution, where
his contact with experienced masters may be limited,
risks losing his sense of Dharma identity. Living in a
world far removed from the peaceful Dharma envi-
ronment of Tibet, caught up in constant distractions
and obligations, and forced to confront corrosive cul-
tural influences rooted in ways of life foreign to the
Dharma, he can always fall back on ritual practices
and the routines of monastic life. In time, however, the
link to the deeper level of the teachings may weaken.

Practitioners in Tibet face an entirely different set
of difficulties. With remarkable foresight, lamas in the
1920s and '30s placed unusual emphasis on giving
their students an education in depth, but the mkhan-
pos now in their prime had almost no opportunity to
study in this way. A few masters of the older generation, grown strong through overcoming hardships
and restrictions, have managed to pass on their understanding, but these are rare cases. Anyone looking at

these circumstances will inevitably feel grave concern. The richness and depth of Tibetan traditions of knowledge are being lost, and the vigorous discipline that helped mold serious practitioners and scholars is fading away.

For Western students who wish to strengthen their connection to the Dharma, the changed situation of Tibetan Buddhism can lead to tremendous uncertainty. For instance, how can they decide with whom to study? Knowing that a lama holds an important incarnation lineage may not offer much guidance, for although there are lineages in which almost every master has demonstrated remarkable qualities, many lineage holders seem to be very ordinary persons. As in any tradition, some who profess to be teachers are not qualified to act as they do, and in these disordered times, the old institutional safeguards that prevented abuse are no longer available. Initially it may be enough to know that a teacher upholds the Mantrayāna, but in time serious students must get clear on the approach a teacher cultivates and invites in his students. Otherwise it is possible to end up uncertain what course to follow, how to develop one's practice, and where to place one's faith.

The relation between teacher and student is in any case a difficult issue for most Westerners. Buddhism teaches that we are not our consciousness or beliefs; that the mind is like a hat we wear, and that no one wears the hat. Coming to see the truth of these teachings requires learning to go beyond identification with self-image and identity, and traditionally it falls to the teacher to communicate this most vital teaching. The teacher works with the student to challenge self and ego, calling into question every position and defense that the self musters to uphold its limited way of being. But Westerners have great difficulties with this model. Trained to be independent, they tend to think they can find their own way. If they remain firm in this conviction, they only reinforce the hold of what they already understand.

It is up to teacher and student alike to work with this fundamental obstacle. If teachers do not take on their traditional role, relying instead on personal charisma to keep students involved, or simply giving their students what they want, how long will their Dharma work endure? If students settle for approaches that conform to their projections, looking to the teacher simply for inspiration, the good experiences and insights they cherish may not have a lasting impact.

Westerners certainly have the potential for deep understanding of Buddhist teachings. But just as a young bride eager to have children must go through pregnancy and the pain of labor, so Dharma students will gain knowledge only through strong commitment and intensive effort that go well beyond what the self finds comfortable.

Limits on Western
Knowledge of Dharma

It is natural for Western Dharma students to look to other Westerners for guidance. They have ample opportunity to do so, for today many Western students who have studied with Buddhist teachers are sharing their discoveries through workshops and in books, and a visit to any bookstore will show that Buddhism has become a popular subject in the self-help market. In the academic world, Buddhist studies remains a fairly obscure specialty, but there has been an important shift, for many in the new generation of scholars have a personal interest in Buddhism, and some even complement their academic studies with traditional forms of practice.

Because they often dedicate themselves to careful study of Dharma texts, scholars are good candidates for bringing a deeper understanding of Dharma to this culture. However, many forces work against this positive potential. Drawn to the teachings that seem the most intellectually challenging, Western scholars may turn early in their careers to the study or translation of works that in Tibet were reserved for advanced practitioners. Unwilling or unable to complete the traditional course of training, they explore Dharma topics in their own way, making gaps in their knowledge inevitable. When they choose particular texts or themes to work with, they often lack the time to explore different commentaries on a word-by-word basis over a period of many months, or lack access to a Tibetan master willing to guide them so intensively.

The appropriate master may not be easy to find, for even a lama said to be a master of Sūtra and Tantra may not be expert in the distinctive explanations of each school or all the texts related to every subject. The need for a genuine knowledge-holder is even more pressing for Tantric materials. For the tantras, the explicator must know the mTha'-drug and the Tshul-bzhi, the Six Limits and the Four Ways of Explanation; he must also understand the four levels of meaning of any single word: tshig-don, the literal meaning; spyi-don, the general meaning; sbas-don, the hidden meaning; and mthar-thug-gi-don, the final definitive meaning. Without this essential background, subtleties of interpretation—the different approaches of different schools, disputed points, lineages of interpretation, the historical context for a debated term or concept—may be lost.

Some of these difficulties might be overcome if scholars engaged in ongoing dialogue aimed at refining their skills and understanding. But academic debates often seem based more on criticism and defensiveness than on a search for mutual insight. Forced to make a career of their expertise and eager to make a name for themselves, scholars may be tempted to act as though they know more than they do. Rewarded for staking out positions at odds with traditional understanding, they can easily discard approaches they have not fully explored. And while the academic way of playing with words and ideas can be stimulating, it can also create obstacles if it is not combined with in-depth knowledge and heartfelt appreciation for the value of the teachings.

In making these remarks, I do not mean to discourage either scholars or students. My purpose is to encourage and support a careful approach to the Dharma by pointing out possible dangers. Western mind is ordinary worldly mind, shaped by a samsaric way of perceiving and the momentum of the eight worldly dharmas. Accordingly, authentic understanding that would let scholars formulate Dharma concepts and expressions suitable for communicating to others can take root only with great difficulty.

This same difficulty has emerged throughout history whenever the Dharma is transmitted from one civilization to another. But to become vividly aware of this 'obvious' dilemma is not so easy; to remain in the uncomfortable place of acknowledging not-knowing and questioning one's own certainties is a serious ongoing practice. Just such a practice is the best way to protect against distortion. The point is to take special care, so that a good foundation is laid for the future of the Dharma in the West.

Difficulties of Translation

Whether they study with a traditional teacher or not, most Westerners must depend on translations to gain access to the teachings. Yet Buddhist texts, with their experiential foundation and rich history of interpretation, present translators with an almost impossible challenge. How can a translation stay true to the meaning of the original while giving access to an audience trained in a different way of thinking? The problem operates at the most basic level, for even such established terms as 'wisdom' (for 'prajñā') or 'enlightenment' or 'transcendence' may not be able to hold the truth of the original.

A standard translation such as 'emptiness' for 'śūnyatā' simply cannot capture the sixteen, eighteen, or twenty ways of expressing the truth of śūnyatā developed in the 8,000-Line, 25,000-Line, and 100,000-Line Prajñāpāramitā Sūtras; it cannot hold the weight of Nāgārjuna's removal of thirty-two types of exaggeration and denigration (sgro-'dogs so-gnyis).The negation implicit in the English 'empty' cannot fulfill the requirements of the chen-po stong-pa-nyid or the rnam-kun mchog-ldan-gyi stong-pa-nyid. Even a glimpse of the meaning of 'śūnya' and 'tā' and 'śūnyatā' would require a thorough course of Sūtrayāna study, including such texts as the Abhisamayālaṁkāra of Miatreya and the Prasannapadā of Candrakīrti.

Scholars who undertake translation may be well trained by Western standards, but whether their training prepares them for the task at hand is open to question. Doctoral students often receive an intensive but narrow education. The emphasis on early specialization makes it difficult to obtain the required depth and breadth of background to understand the subtleties of any texts they set out to translate. Even the development of proficiency in one or more canonical languages is no guarantee of accuracy. After all, a native speaker fluent in Tibetan who has memorized many Dharma texts is not automatically qualified to comment on great Buddhist works.

In Tibet, students understood that each field of study had its own vocabulary, and that a single term could change its meaning completely depending on the context. For example, stong-pa and snang-ba, which can be translated in casual terms as 'emptiness' and 'appearance', have different connotations in each of the four philosophical schools. Translating sgrib-pa as 'obscuration' may fit for the terms 'nyon-mongs-pa'i sgrib-pa' and 'shes-bya'i sgrib-pa', but not for 'snyoms-'jug-gi sgrib-pa'. 'rTen-'brel' in the Sūtrayāna texts does not mean what it does in Mantrayāna texts. When the term 'tha-mal-gyi shes-pa' is translated as 'simplicity mind of nowness', which of the three kinds of tha-mal-gyi shes-pa does the translator think he is translating—gNyugs-sems-tha-mal-gyi-shes-pa, ma-bcos-tha-mal-gyi-shes-pa, or khrul-sems-tha-mal-gyi-shes-pa?

Whether a term is used in a text regarded as drang-don rather than nges-don might radically change the way it should be translated into English. If Tathāgata-garbha is said to be rtag-pa, does 'rtag-pa' mean 'permanent' as opposed to 'impermanent'; or does it suggest 'everlasting beyond time'? In order to convey the original in full context, one needs to know how a text is regarded by different schools. Again, context can change meaning drastically. For example, the philosophical term 'spros-bral' has been mistranslated as 'simplicity' by reference to a completely different context: 'spros-bcas' (elaborate) and 'spros-med' (simple) used to refer to the degree of complexity involved in rituals or empowerments.

If scholars are able to get clear about the precise meaning of the Tibetan term in context, they may still not be able to find the suitable English. If they lack training in their own philosophical traditions, or if they are not familiar with the roots of English words and their philosophical usages at different times in history, they may miss the distinctive flavor or connotation of a particular English term. If they do not study the shifting meanings of a term like 'awareness' in Western texts by different authors or from different disciplines, they may unwittingly introduce mis-understandings. Even when scholars work closely with Tibetans, difficulties in communication may still arise, for rarely is a Tibetan master well versed in the subtle aspects of Western thought.

Enlightened masters like Padmasambhava, Tilopa, or 'Jam-dbyangs mKhyen-brtse have a direct way of transforming the student's understanding without the need for words. The early Tibetan translators went through a rigorous training, guided by such highly qualified masters, who worked with them intensively over a period of years. To assure the accuracy of their work, they deepened their understanding of the texts through intensive study and practice. Gradually a standard vocabulary and ways of phrasing were codified for the use of those who would come later. This method has proved its worth, for translations done twelve centuries ago have required only minor revisions since.

A good model is Vairotsana, the eighth century Tibetan master, who learned through dedicated study with many masters how to judge the significance of what the texts presented. He became a master translator, fitting Tibetan to the innermost meaning of the texts and the needs and understanding of the audience. He translated essential works of the Sūtrayāna, major texts of the Mantrayāna, and many śāstras, and his work influenced others for generations to come.

In the West, translators follow a different model. They cultivate their own style and understanding, true to the Tibetan saying, "Each horse has its own gait." Some may elaborate on the original, looking for poetic forms of expression or adding layers of interpretation.

Others may struggle to stay close to the source, but end up adopting words and phrases that convey little meaning to a Western audience. Still others may borrow words from philosophical traditions such as phenomenology or logic with little grounds for confidence that the new term, torn from its original context, will serve the purpose. The results can be especially unfortunate when translators who lack in-depth understanding and linguistic mastery produce works that become well established. In that case, their misunderstandings can easily become dogma for the next generation of scholars and practitioners.

These problems might be surmountable if accomplished Tibetan masters worked closely with translators, yet this rarely happens. Determined to spread the Dharma widely, many Tibetan teachers seem more ready to present ideas in simple, immediate ways than deal with complications that earlier masters would have investigated in depth. In addition, Tibetans must cope with the temporal pressures of the modern world. In the past, it generally took at least twenty years to gain a comprehensive education. Today some students receive the degree of mkhan-po after just five years of study. It is difficult to believe that such an accelerated pace could lead to real mastery.

My own view is that translators should proceed cautiously, mastering issues of language before jumping into issues of meaning, and allow their deepening appreciation for the meaning of a text to inform their inquiry into language. In a democracy, everyone is entitled to his or her own opinion, and so I will express mine: The terminology and understanding of translators at present is not adequate to convey certain meanings of the Dharma. Tibetan teachers and Western scholars alike have a responsibility to work toward greater accuracy and standardized vocabularies. This process may take several generations, but without such discipline, how can the meaning be preserved?

Tibetan masters may wonder whether such rigor is necessary, since relatively few Westerners are interested in the philosophical side of Buddhism. Perhaps it would help if they had a clearer sense of the treatment religion has received in the West. Western philosophers and scientists, steeped in materialist views, have long attacked the tenets of Christianity. One day they will turn their skeptical forms of inquiry to Buddhism, posing logical objections and seeking out contradictions. A small joke, a kindly smile, or a cryptic response will not stem such objections. Without real and convincing explanations, Buddhism will find itself confined to small circles of believers who share a similar rhetoric, and its power to bring about transformation will be placed in jeopardy.

PART THREE

Daily Dharma

Approaches to the Dharma

Through the kindness of my teachers, I arrived in this country with a certain knowledge of the scriptures, holding the lineage for many important teachings. Yet I very soon realized that I could not simply transmit this knowledge in traditional ways, and I began to explore alternate approaches for students to engage the Dharma. Over time our community has developed its own way of practicing, its own path. The heart of this path is work.

For students of Dharma ready to study the operation of samsara and challenge the patterns of illusion mind, work reveals the mind in action. At first students may think of their jobs simply in terms of producing results, but as they cope with the challenges that work involves—time pressure, lack of knowledge, frustration, negative emotions—students begin to develop the clear sense that they are on a path. The discipline of getting up early, working late, and staying focused throughout the day lets them watch the rhythms of the mind, day in and day out. Working with mindfulness and a strong focus on doing their best, investigating through their work who they are and how their minds function, they are following the path of inquiry laid down in the ancient Sūtras and śāstras. Without emphasizing formal study, initiations, or ceremonies, they are connecting with the lineage of realization.

By responding to the challenge of producing results, students learn that the mind can be changed. Using their hands and heads, they see what it is like to discipline the mind and to care. They see how commitment turns frustration into patience; how concentration turns confusion into clarity. Focused on action and on being productive, they can confront emotional ups and downs, challenge unwanted patterns, and develop endurance, flexibility, and stability. Those who enter our community start for personal reasons, but those who stay develop a love for this way of working and the way of life it supports.

Learning through
Serving the Dharma

When our organization began, almost no one had real knowledge of the Dharma. Over the years, we have learned by doing, by making a contribution. We have learned the fundamentals of Buddhist history and thought by writing about them, learned to open to the power of Buddhist symbols by creating them, learned an appreciation for the Tibetan language by producing Tibetan books. More fundamental still, we have learned how to follow the path by honoring commitments and letting our intention shape our conduct. The results we get teach us faith in disciplined work, a faith well suited to the Western mind, since it is grounded in tangible accomplishments and can be deepened through our own efforts

Within the structures we have put in place to ensure good results, we have the freedom to learn for ourselves. Each day we practice karma yoga: the disciplines of patience, effort, sensitivity toward others, and work not directed at personal benefit. Each day we demonstrate through our accomplishments the value of what Buddhism can offer the world. What has been accomplished by a small group of people is truly amazing.

As we work, we make connections to the Dharma and to the lineage; as we create, something deep is being created within us. If we try, we can learn; if we learn, we can benefit ourselves and others. Once we are on track, the discipline we need—like virtue itself—comes naturally. The mandala enters into us, and we become part of the mandala.

Westerners come to the Dharma with certain advantages. Many are intelligent and open-minded and start with good motivation. Heirs to a tradition that fought to establish freedom of religion, they can practice Dharma without official opposition. Familiar with the Western lifestyle, they can see through Western versions of the samsaric dream. Having inherited a tradition of hard work and technology put to good use, they can take on major projects with the potential to benefit future generations of Westerners and Tibetans alike.

I have tried my best to build on these advantages. For instance, we have typeset, printed, and distributed to Tibetans hundreds of thousands of volumes of Tibetan texts. Perhaps a thousand Tibetan Buddhist centers have directly benefited. Some may question the value of this contribution, arguing that knowledge of these texts is almost lost. But my teachers taught me that the words of the Buddhas and great masters were precious. As long as there are mkhan-pos and lamas to read and cherish them, we will make any effort necessary.

Some may imagine that in America such accomplishments come easily, but those of us who have given so much of our life's energy to getting these results know otherwise. Yet the benefits for my students have also been great. Our community knows now that behind each manifestation of the Buddhadharma stands a long lineage and a rich, deeply significant history. Many students have developed strong skills and a certain level of understanding. Perhaps some will become teachers. Whatever they do, they will find ways to express and develop their understanding of the Nyingma tradition. Even for students who leave the community, the connection with the lineage, and the opportunity to share in some small way its blessings, endures.

Through our work, we have created Dharma forms and symbols that make the teachings available, contributions that will endure long after we are gone. Half of our work goes to support the Sangha in Asia and half of it is for America and the West, seeds planted for the long term. Living amidst sacred symbols that support our practice, we are helping transmit the Dharma to a new culture. Introducing the mandala of Kāya, Vaca, and Citta to a new land, we have come to embody some of this value in our own hearts, and we can take satisfaction in having a physical witness to our time on earth. If we had spent thirty years in study and retreat, would we have achieved as much?

Through our work, we have learned the importance of discipline. Seeing the results we have produced, our motivation grows stronger and our strength is renewed. Each of us contributes, maximizing what can be accomplished. We have found a way to guarantee that we do not waste our lives or cheat ourselves by living in fantasy and expectation. As shape becomes form and form comes alive, as the Dharma manifests outward, we are learning to see with Dharma eyes.

Through the fruits of our work, a new vision has taken form within us. As we practice transforming laziness and ignorance into crystal awareness, we are becoming worker-philosophers, embodying our knowledge and transmitting it through the forms we bring into being. We do not expect to be a model for others, for we are simply getting started on a project that will continue for generations. Yet we can be proud of our participation in the mandala of accomplishment. Such pride does not feed the self: It helps us develop beyond it. It makes self and self-concerns transparent.

Making Mind the Matter

A s the members of our community go about their
work, they try to keep the goal of understanding
the teachings close to their hearts and minds. We are
looking for ways to make the Dharma relevant to our
minds and to explore the activity of our minds in light
of the Dharma.

Traditionally, such practice is linked to śīla,
samādhi, and prajñā. The three trainings help us see
how samsara is fabricated and by whom, and what
patterns of ego, personality, and identity have been
put in place as a result. Each training gives access to a
different body of knowledge. Śīla is the body of
knowledge that prevents further fabrication, samādhi
the body of knowledge that transforms what has been
fabricated, and prajñā the body of knowledge that
reveals how the fabrication comes to be.

With prajñā comes insight into the Four Noble
Truths. Seeing reality as it is, we shift our focus from
the problems that concern us as human beings to the
root problem: mind itself. Investigating the operation
of the kleśas and the feelings of confusion, neediness,
and insecurity they generate, we discover how our
ways of sensing and experiencing cooperate to create
and manifest suffering.

Taking work as Dharma practice gives us the opportunity to pursue a similar kind of inquiry. In work we can investigate experience as it happens. What matters is learning to identify self and self-image in operation, always going on to ask another question instead of settling for a particular understanding. Here are some suggestions, based on my own observations, on ways to do this.

Examining the Senses   It may seem that our senses operate in a neutral way, but that is only because we have not learned to look closely. Just as science has learned to investigate in depth the atoms and molecules that make up matter, so we can learn to look at how we see and hear and feel and know. Rather than focusing on what appears to the senses, we can be aware of the activity of sensing, and of the way we react to what we sense.

There are many ways to conduct this inquiry. For instance, instead of focusing on objects, we can be aware of space as the background from which objects appear. Instead of accepting the way things are, we can determine how appearance develops through a series of transitions that unfold in time. Instead of accepting the identity of what is sensed, we can ask how our own reactions and sense of self-identity contribute to the feel and flavor of appearance.

The Changing River   Like a river, experience is never the same from one moment to the next, but we tend to ignore change and emphasize similarity. Insisting that the past has gone and the future has not yet come, we turn the present into something static: a fixed and rigid identity. To counter this tendency, we can focus in our experience on how things change from moment to moment. Right now I think I am the same person that I was last year or five minutes ago, but in fact the mind, feelings, and desires are constantly changing. Instead of insisting on sameness, can we simply appreciate the subtle differences?

We sometimes worry that we can't see the forest for the trees, but the opposite is also true: Once we have identified the forest, we find it hard to notice the twigs, the leaves, the branches, the birds, and the rustling underfoot. The Abhidharma offers the tools for analyzing subtle changes in the mind and learning to notice different levels of cognition and perception. Mantrayāna teachings and the samādhis take this analysis to still more subtle levels. But daily experience can be a preparation for these more advanced approaches. Right now we can notice changes in experience and trace the consequences of such changes, and we can experiment with modifying or initiating changes on our own.

Beyond Samsaric Mind Beginning meditators usually focus on calming the mind or simply observing experience. This is natural, since our thoughts and imagination give us so much trouble. But tending to mind and mental events the way a shepherd tends his sheep is inherently limiting. We may meditate in this way for years without a significant change in how mind operates. Ironically, the self that fixates on its mental projections knows little about how those projections arise and operate. When we always meditate in this way—in preventive mode—we cannot add to this store of knowledge.

Instead of staying focused on the content of illusion mind, we can investigate the body of mind. To really succeed at this means cultivating samādhi and prajñā, but we can also conduct an initial and rewarding investigation in the midst of ordinary experience. All we need to do is learn to recognize our own projections and preconceptions in operation. Like a spider who gets caught in its own web, we are constantly getting trapped in structures that the mind sets up. If we can see this pattern in operation, we can become more aware of how the mind works, and this will make it easier to work with mind itself.

Multiple Experience   Whatever we experience, there is also the one who experiences and interprets. As we interpret, we are also offering a self-interpretation. Like our sensings, our interpretations go in two directions at once, and we can practice being aware of both at the same time.

We can also go further into the complications of mind. As mind projects outward, it is confirming preconceptions, adjusting its own role and activity, and assigning and refining meaning. In every moment of experience, it goes off in many directions, like a ray of light split into many colors by a prism. It is not easy to keep track of all this, but at least we can make a start. Sense experience is a good place to look, because it is so immediate. We can develop a sensitivity to the manifold directionality of experience that might otherwise be too complicated to observe.

Following Experience into Aliveness Although investigating our own experience leads us into the realm of interpretation, it does not have to lead us away from the richness that experience holds. Interpretation is just another layer of experience, with its own aliveness. Similarly, minding, sensing, cognizing, and identifying are all richly alive, each in its own way. A sound is made and a meaning pronounced; self-image and identity emerge to name and define what has been experienced; the senses gather together to make more meanings. It is a mistake to think that all of this happens *after* experience has taken place. Instead, each of these steps is part of the living experience, available to inquiry.

If we let the aliveness of mind's interpretations and mindings guide us toward an understanding of how experience is identified and assigned significance, we can take a further step, noticing how mind's way of patterning repeats itself again and again. Different features appear, but the rhetoric of minding and sensing stays the same. Even in dreams, the rhythm of mind in operation is never once interrupted.

Staying with the Unknown Like quicksilver, the mind is never at rest, and like quicksilver it slips away when we try to take hold of it or penetrate beneath its surface. Always sensing, always interpreting, mind goes its own way. It makes meaning even where there is no meaning. What resists being assigned meaning, what stays unknown, is dismissed as irrelevant and of no value.

One way to challenge these tendencies is to let the unknown stay unknown. At once certain aspects of experience become more accessible: balance and neutrality, being open, and allowing. Staying with the experience of not knowing allows us to ask questions that would otherwise be dismissed. For instance, does form arise from ignorance or from wisdom? The mind at once leaps in with an answer, but this is only at the level of stories. If we can let ourselves not know the answer, we can explore the question at a deeper level, asking within experience instead of taking a stand on experience. We can see how well we understand mind · itself, and we can ask how mind relates to mind.

Intrinsic Certainty   As we go about minding our stories, what are we certain of? Can we investigate this question without depending on stories? Can we go to a depth of certainty deeper than any story, deeper than the conditions we set for understanding? These questions pose a challenge. As long as we rely on identification and interpretation we may not even be able to say what they mean. Still, once we discover a way to start looking, it does not matter where we head. Every direction leads us into the depth of mind.

Knowing our Solidity   Beneath the particular story in effect right now, we rely on an identity that feels solid. We simply know we are one mind, one consciousness. If we can go to that level, where everything seems solid, the notions and assumptions we use to shape experience—our ordinary way of thinking—may look different. Even our ideas about awareness, mind, consciousness, and experience may present themselves differently, revealing other features of mind.

Caring Brings Understanding To understand, we must care. When we care, we are not disturbed by the obstacles that arise on the path to understanding, and we easily overcome emotionality. The Dharma tells us that if we love and care for knowledge, then by taking the path of knowledge, we come to know how to love and care for ourselves. We take responsibility for what we can bring about in this life, and we set about eliminating confusion and other hindrances that prevent mind and self from functioning at their full potential.

This kind of caring does not depend on being ready to undertake serious study of the Dharma. It is enough to see that we are the cause of our own experience, for then we can look for ways to cultivate whatever is positive. If we make it our aim to contribute and to experience as fully as possible, we will inevitably realize that our own knowledge is not sufficient to guide us, and we will explore ways to improve it. If we feel some connection to the Dharma lineage, we may recognize that today there are fewer and fewer examples of individuals who manifest profound knowledge in their own lives. In our own small way, we may resolve to do what we can to become examples of knowledge and caring for our friends, through simple acts such as kind words and helping gestures.

Although it is hard to claim that we can manifest complete honesty and compassion toward ourselves and others, we can imitate the examples of those we admire and whose lives we study. Whether we call this working for the Dharma or working for ourselves, we live in a way that does not waste the opportunities we have been given. We shape our own karma.

Mind is always dealing with the matter at hand, the 'stuff' out of which its stories are constructed. But mind matters more than the subject-matter of its stories. If we care about knowledge, we will see this, because real knowledge happens at a level different from the stories we tell. If we care about ourselves, we will tire of our suffering and realize through our inquiry that we could do it differently; that mind could wake up from the stories it tells and recognize them as fictions.

Mind is always asking, "What's the matter?" But if we let go of what matters to mind; if we let mind be what matters, we can release ourselves from the hold of what mind tells us matters most. In time, we may realize what is the matter with mind. If what matters to mind has never happened, the problems we take so seriously dissolve. The rules of the game display less gravity; the limits on the range of positions available to us fall away. We can tell the story of how mind manufactures reality, or the story of how we have arrived at realization. Either way, it doesn't matter.

Appendices

Glossary

*This glossary lists terms in the text that are mentioned but
not defined, or defined once but used more than once. Terms
defined in the text and not repeated are not included. Where
possible, definitions have been taken from the text itself.
Other definitions have been adapted from discussions found
in other books written or edited under the direction of
Tarthang Tulku. Where terms are left undefined, references
are given to discussion in the text. Unless otherwise indi-
cated, the Sanskrit term precedes the Tibetan.*

Abhidharma, mngon chos   Teachings compiled from
the teachings of the Buddha that analyze the nature of
what is; one of the collections of the Tripiṭaka.

Ālaya, kun gzhi   The all-ground consciousness.

Ālayavijnana, kun-gzhi rnam-shes   The all-ground
conscious that has begun to stir, activating the process
leading to conventional consciousness and appearance.

Aprapañca, spros bral   Freedom from prapañca.

Arhat, dgra bcom-pa   One who has attained realization by breaking through the bondage of emotional
obscurations.

Atiyoga, rdzogs-chen   The highest teachings according to the Nyingma tradition. The term means 'great
perfection' or great completion.' Its divisions include
sems sde, klong sde, and man ngag gi sde.

Avādanas, rtog brjod   Accounts of past lives of the Buddha's disciples that teach the value and benefits of action in accordance with the Dharma.

Avalokiteśvara   The Great Bodhisattva who exemplifies the practice of compassion and stands always available to bring benefit to others.

Bardo   Intermediate state; usually refers to the interim between death and rebirth.

Bhūmis   The (ten) stages of the Bodhisattva path.

Blo sbyong   The practice of training or purifying the mind. The blo-sbyong teachings were introduced into Tibet by Atiśa. They are taught in all schools of Tibetan Buddhism.

Bodhicitta, byang-chub kyi sems (sems-bskyed)   The heart and mind of the Bodhisattva, vast in compassion and deep in wisdom.

Bodhisattva, byang-chub sems-dpa'   One who bases his practice on bodhicitta, generating the intention to lead all beings to enlightenment.

Buddha, sangs-rgyas   The Enlightened One, who has fully awakened and has accomplished all that must be accomplished. The Buddha manifests in three aspects, known as the three kāya.

Bying-ba   A lost, fuzzy state that can be confused with zhi-gnas.

Cig-car gyis-pa   (The mind) that realizes at once.

Citta, sems In general, the mind. As as aspect of Buddha nature, it refers to enlightened awareness.

Dharmadhātu, chos kyi dbyings Literally, the realm of Dharma.

Dharmakāya, chos-sku An aspect or 'embodiment' of the Buddha that could be referred to as absolute Buddha nature.

Dharmatā, chos-nyid The 'isness' of all that is.

sDom-pa bzhi Four statements that summarize the Buddha's teachings: all that is compounded is impermanent; all that is defiled with emotionality is suffering; all dharmas are empty; nirvana is peace.

Drang-don (Skt. neyārtha) Meaning that requires further explanation.

rDzogs-chen See Atiyoga.

Eight worldly dharmas The basis for attachment to the patterns of hope and fear. They constitute four pairs: praise and blame, gain and loss, fame and disgrace, and happiness and suffering.

Five Aspects of the Enlightened Ones In highly simplified terms, body, speech, mind, qualities, and enlightened activity. (In Tibetan: sku, gsung, thugs, yon-tan, and phrin-las).

Five Paths See under Path.

Four Foundations for Mindfulness Body, feelings, mind, and Dharma.

Four Meditative Stages (in Madhyamaka)   Emptiness (bden-med), unity (zung-'jug), aprapañca (spros-bral), and equality (mnyam-nyid).

Four Stages of Yoga (according to sGam-po-pa)   One pointedness (rtse-gcig), aprapañca (spros-bral), one taste (ro-cig), and non-meditation (sgom-med). Each stage has three divisions (che-'bring chung gsum).

Four Noble Truths   The truth of universal suffering, the source of suffering, the cessation of suffering, and the path to that cessation.

Garuḍa   A noble mythic bird, giant in stature, with divine attributes: the vehicle of Indra.

God realm   One of the six realms in which beings wander in samsara, characterized by delights and pleasures that continue until shortly before the end of existence in that realm. There are many god realms.

rGod-pa   A kind of excitement that can be confused with wakefulness.

Hell realm   One of the six realms in which beings wander in samsara, characterized by endless suffering. There are eight hot and eight cold hell realms.

Jātakas   Accounts of the Buddha's virtuous conduct in past lives that teach the value and benefits of action in accordance with the Dharma.

Jñāna, ye-shes   Awakened wisdom.

Jñeyavaraṇa, shes-bya'i sgrib-pa   Cognitive obscurations to enlightenment created by mind.

Kalpa, bskal-pa An inconceivably long period of time.

Karma and kleśa, las and nyon-mongs The behavior patterns and emotionalities that give mind's fabrications their momentum and sustain our steady refusal to see through what mind presents.

Kāya The aspect of the Buddha related to physical manifestation.

mKhan-po (Skt. upadhyāya) Title conferred on one who has completed the basic course of study, which traditionally lasted at least ten years.

Kleśa See karma and kleśa.

Kleśavaraṇa, nyon-mongs kyi sgrib Emotionally toned obscurations to enlightenment created by mind.

Kṣitigarbha One of the Eight Great Bodhisattvas, who takes special care of those suffering in the hell realms.

Madhyamaka, dbu-ma Teachings known as the Middle Way, presented by Nāgārjuna as a way of clarifying the Prajñāpāramitā. The philosophical school that developed on the basis of Nāgārjuna's teachings is known as the Mādhyamika. The term dBu-ma chen-po refers to specific teachings cultivated in Tibet known as the Great Madhyamaka.

Mahā, Anu, and Atiyoga The three inner yogas in the Nyingma tradition. They correspond to the three inner Tantras and the final three of the nine yānas recognized in Nyingma teachings.

Mahāmudrā, phyag-rgya chen-po   The highest teachings in the Kagyud tradition. The term means Great Symbol: the ultimate symbol that includes all others.

Mahāyāna   The Great Vehicle: the path followed by those who have awakened Bodhicitta and entered the path of the Bodhisattva. It includes the Sūtrayāna or Bodhisattvayāna and the Mantrayāna or Vajrayāna.

Maitreya   The future Buddha, who will appear when the time is once more ripe to make the path to liberation available to all beings.

Mañjuśrī   Manifestation of enlightened wisdom. The Bodhisattva who cuts through all illusion and reveals the inner truth of reality.

Mantra   An instrument for the transformation of the mind through the energies associated with speech.

Mantrayāna, rgyud-kyi theg-pa   The vehicle that uses the science of mantra to illuminate the path to enlightenment, followed by those who practice the skillful means taught in the Tantras.

Nges-don (Skt. nitārtha)   Meaning that is absolutely certain and requires no further explication.

dNgos-po and dngos-med   The two opposites of existence and non-existence.

Nirvana, mya ngan las 'das   The extinction of samsara.

Nisvabhava, rang-bzhin med-pa   Not having been born or come into being.

Nyams Exceptional meditative experiences such as bliss, peace, clarity, and wakefulness.

Paramārthasatya, don-dam bden-pa Absolute truth: the level at which the conventional realm has never come into being.

Pariniṣpanna, kun-rdzob bden-pa Everyday, conventional truth.

Path of Preparation, tshogs-lam First of the five paths that make up the path to enlightenment.

Path of Linking, sbyor-lam The second of the five paths that links preparation to insight and realization. It has four levels, known as heat, summit, patience, and supreme worldly dharmas.

Path of Seeing, mthong-lam The third of the five paths; the path on which insight into the nature of reality arises and the Bodhisattva path begins.

Path of Meditation, bsgom-lam The fourth path, in which one cultivates and matures what has been recognized on the path of seeing.

Path of No More Learning, mi-slob-pa'i-lam The fifth of the five paths, followed by the Buddhas, who alone among all beings are fully accomplished.

dPe-yi ye-shes The clarity of śūnyatā, involving a seeing that is direct but in the manner of inference.

Pointing-out instructions See discussion at pp. 52–59.

Prajñā, shes-rab   The symbolic name for a transcending, awakened awareness, a higher, intrinsic all knowing knowledge that is beyond naming, beyond the senses, and beyond thinking. The body of knowledge that reveals how the fabrications of samsaric mind come to be.

Prajñāpāramitā, shes-rab kyi pha-rol tu phyin-pa The teaching of complete omniscience, constituting the heart of the Buddha's realization, associated with the Second Turning.

Prapañca, spros pa   The dynamic that oscillates ceaselessly between one limiting view and its opposite.

Pratītyasamutpāda, rten-'brel   The teaching of interdependent cooperation, showing how samsara arises through mutual interactions that can be analyzed into twelve links.

Pratyekabuddha, rang sangs-rgyas A solitary Buddha, who attains enlightenment through contemplation of pratītyasamutpāda and does not teach.

Rim-gyis-pa   (The mind) that develops in stages.

Sādhana, sgrub   Ritual practice and its related texts.

Śākyamuni Buddha   The historical Buddha, the Sage of the Sakya clan.

Samādhi, ting-nge-'dzin   One of the three trainings. The body of practice and knowledge that focuses on conduct, transforming what mind has fabricated.

Śamatha and vipaśyanā, zhi-gnas and lhag-mthong
Forms of meditative practice. Śamatha brings calm to
the wild energies of mind. Vipaśyanā clarifies the confusion created by ignorance.

Samsara The spinning wheel of illusion and delusion, of endless transmigration and uninterrupted agitation, that drives our being.

Samvṛtisatya, kun-rdzob bden-pa Everyday conventional truth, which accepts what appears and
claims to exist as being real.

Sangha The community of those who commit themselves to practicing the teachings of the Buddha.

Sarvadharma, chos thams-cad The truth of the entire
field of reality and experience.

Sarvāstivādins Followers of one of the original
eighteen schools of Buddhism that formed in the centuries after the Buddha. Noted for emphasizing study
of Abhidharma, they gave rise to the philosophical
school known as the Vaibhāśika.

Śāstras Commentaries on the teachings of the
Buddha written by the enlightened masters of India.

Sems-nyid Literally but misleadingly 'mind-as-such'
or 'mindness'; for a discussion, see pp. 36–37, 49–50.

Siddha, grub-pa An accomplished yogin who has
mastered the power of mind.

Śīla, tshul-khrims   One of the three trainings. The body of practice and knowledge that focus on awareness, preventing further mental fabrication.

Six Perfections   The transcendent practices of the Bodhisattva who has vowed to become a Buddha: giving, moral conduct, patience, intense effort, concentration, and wisdom.

Śrāvaka, nyan-thos   A follower of the First Turning teachings; literally, one who has heard the teachings and accepts them.

Śūnyatā, stong-pa-nyid   A term often but misleadingly translated as 'emptiness' or 'complete openness'; see discussion at pp. 27–31 and 84.

Sūtra, mdo   The Buddha's teachings on the nature of ground, path, and goal. They dispel all doubt, awaken faith, and lay the foundation for samādhi.

Sūtrayāna, mdo'i theg-pa   The Mahāyāna path that relies on the Sūtras and on the practice of the Six or Ten Perfections.

Ten Stages (bhūmi, sa)   The ten levels of practice for one who has entered the Bodhisattva path. The Bodhisattva enters the first stage on the Path of Seeing, the third of the Five Paths.

Theravādin   Followers of the Buddha's teachings in the lands of Southeast Asia. They maintain a Vinaya lineage descending directly from the Buddha and follow First Turning teachings.

Thirty-Seven Wings Aspects of the path to enlightenment: the four foundations of mindfulness, the four genuine restraints, the four bases of supernatural powers, the five spiritual faculties, the five spiritual powers, the seven branches of enlightenment, and the eightfold path.

Three Excellences (Treasures) Bodhicitta as basic motivation; the central practice, performed with the whole heart; and dedication of the merit.

Three Trainings Śīla, samādhi, and prajñā. The trainings work together, preparing the mind to understand the mind.

Three Turnings A classification of the teachings of the Buddha. For a description, see pp. 14–15.

Tirthika A non-Buddhist; one who maintains non-Buddhist views

rTogs (Skt. adhigama) Realization.

gTor-ma Offering cakes presented to deities in the course of ritual.

Tripiṭaka, sde-snod gsum The threefold collection of the Buddha's teachings, consisting of Vinaya, Sūtra, and Abhidharma.

Triple Gem Buddha, Dharma, and Sangha as objects of refuge.

rTon-pa bzhi The Four Reliances; see p. 32.

Vaca   The aspect of the Buddha related to speech and to communication.

Vidyā, rig-pa   Knowledge or spontaneous aware-ness, with no trace of dualistic thought.

Vinaya, 'dul-ba   Teachings that support the growth of moral conduct and codify rules for the guidance of the monastic community and lay people.

Vipaśyanā   See śamatha and vipaśyanā.

Yāna, theg-pa   One of the three (or nine) vehicles that followers of the Dharma mount in order to follow the path to enlightenment. The three yānas are tradition-ally described as Śrāvakayāna, Pratekabuddhayāna, and Mahāyāna.

Yogin, rnal-'byor-pa   A male practitioner who focuses intensively on practice, withdrawing from conven-tional worldly concerns. The female equivalent is yoginī, rnal-'byor-ma.

Masters Mentioned in the Text

Disciples of the Buddha

Rāhula   The son of the Buddha, Rāhula miraculously remained in the womb during the six years the Buddha engaged in the practice of hardships. He was born on the day of the Buddha's enlightenment and was initiated into the monastic order at the age of six by the Buddha's disciple Śāriputra. He later became the Buddha's personal attendant and served him faithfully until the Buddha passed from this life.

Rāhula is said to dwell in the northern region of ancient India, with a retinue of 1,100 Arhats. He holds a diadem that enables devotees to vanquish passion, comprehend the teachings, and receive the blessings of the Buddhas and Bodhisattvas. Those who pray to Rāhula are always watched over by protective deities.

Śāriputra   Born to a brahmin family in Nālandā, Śāriputra was devoted to learning from his youth. With the guidance of his father, a distinguished scholar and well-known teacher, he mastered the traditional sciences and began to tutor his father's students. Together, he and Maudgalyāyana, son of the king's chief minister, left home to study the doctrines and methods of the six most famous spiritual teachers of the time. They were attracted by the honesty of the sixth teacher, who acknowledged that he had yet to find a complete and perfect teaching. This master entrusted his five hundred disciples to their care and directed them to seek out the Sage of the Śākyas.

In time, Śāriputra met one of the Buddha's disciples, a young novice, and attained enlightenment upon hearing him recite the Ye Dharma, a single verse summarizing a central teaching of the Buddha. Śāriputra shared his knowledge with Maudgalyāyana, and the two of them, together with their five hundred disciples, soon joined the community of monks that followed the path set forth by the Buddha. Śāriputra and Maudgalyāyana became the Enlightened One's two foremost disciples and remained with the Buddha until they entered nirvana.

Maudgalyāyana   The son of a learned brahmin, chief minster to the king, Maudgalyāyana received a thorough education in all the classical sciences, with the intention that he would succeed his father. After meeting Śāriputra, however, he decided to follow a religious life. Although his parents at first refused him permission, they relented when they saw him determined to starve rather than abandon his intention.

Maudgalyāyana and Śāriputra became disciples of the same master and took responsibility after his death for his five hundred disciples. They then made a pact: whichever found the truest teaching would immediately share it with the other. When Śāriputra became enlightened upon hearing a verse of the Buddha's teachings, he told Maudgalyāyana of his experience as he had promised. Both of them renounced their last remaining attachments to worldly life and entered the Buddha's Sangha together with their five hundred disciples. Maudgalyāyana became renowned for his yogic insight and psychic powers.

Mahākāśyapa Soon after the Buddha had given his first teaching at the Deer Park in Sārnāth, he stayed at the hermitage of the brahmin Mahākāśyapa, a spiritual master said to be 120 years old. Recognizing the Buddha's superior attainment, Mahākāśyapa entered the order together with his five hundred disciples, accompanied by his two brothers and their 250 disciples. Known as the foremost disciple in ascetic practices, he served the Sangha as the first patriarch after the Buddha entered Parinirvāṇa near Kuśināgara. Soon after the Buddha's passing, he convened the First Council of five hundred Arhats at Rājagṛha to recite and affirm the Buddha's teachings. Then, his work complete, he entered samādhi near the top of a three-peaked mountain. The peaks closed over his body, emtombing him inside. He remains there to this day, awaiting the coming of the Buddha Maitreya.

Subhūti The Arhat Subhūti excelled in understanding of the profound Prajñāpāramitā. When he first withdrew from the world, he took meditation on love as the basis of his practice and soon attained realization. He continued to meditate on loving-kindness whenever he went out on alms rounds before accepting offerings. For this practice he became known as the most excellent among those worthy of offerings.

Subhūti was honored for his special excellence in freeing others from the futility of emotionality and disputation, and was foremost among those who meditate on śūnyatā. In the Prajñāpāramitā Sūtras, Subhūti often serves as the one who questions the Buddha, and through the Buddha's inspiration also offers some of these teachings directly.

Ānanda Son of the Buddha's uncle, Ānanda was among the five hundred Śākyas ordained into the Sangha six years after the Tathāgata's enlightenment. Known as the most devoted of all the Buddha's disciples, he became the Buddha's attendant and heard and remembered his master's every word.

A faithful and loving servant, Ānanda took devotion as his practice and gave little thought to his own enlightenment. Thus, a year after the Blessed One entered Parinirvāṇa, when 499 Arhats gathered to recite the Buddha's teachings, Ānanda was still not an Arhat. Despite the great need for his presence and his knowledge, he could not join them to complete the required number of 500 Arhats. Realizing now that all attachments—even his cherished devotion to the Buddha—must be given up, Ānanda meditated throughout the night and attained enlightenment at dawn the following day. Taking his place among the assembled Arhats, he recited the Sūtras exactly as he had heard the Buddha teach them, so that they could be accurately preserved. He went on to serve the Dharma as the second Patriarch for forty years. then passed away on an island in the Ganges River.

Paṇḍitas

Indrabodhi At the time of the Buddha, the north-western land of Oḍḍiyāna was ruled by King Indrabodhi (also known in some sources as Indra-bhūti), born in the same year as the Enlightened One. One day the king beheld to his amazement a group of monks flying through the sky. Told that they must be disciples of the Buddha, the king determined to invite the Buddha to his kingdom.

The Enlightened One accepted the invitation and flew to meet the king, accompanied by many of his disciples. When Indrabodhi respectfully requested teachings, the Buddha told him that he must start by abandoning all worldly pleasures and attachments. To this Indrabodhi replied that he was too firmly committed to his life as ruler of his people to do this, and asked if there were other methods for one such as him.

Seeing that the king had highly evolved capacities, the Buddha transmitted to him the esoteric Vajrayāna teachings, never before made known in the human realm. As a result of his meritorious attainments in previous lives, the king accomplished the fruit of each teaching as the Buddha revealed it, in the end attaining full and perfect enlightenment.

Many great Dharma kings, including several associated with Oḍḍiyāna, bore the name Indrabodhi or Indrabhūti. The account here relates to the Indrabodhi born at the same time as the Buddha.

Padmasambhava Intending to manifest a miraculous birth to inspire faith in the Dharma and subdue
the fierce deities of Tibet, Amitābha, the Buddha of
Boundless Light, caused a great lotus to arise in the
center of Lake Dhanakoṣa in Oḍḍiyāna, renowned as
the land of the enlightened. Within the lotus appeared
an emanation of Amitābha in the form of an eight-year
old boy. He would become known as Padmasambhava, the Lotus-Born Guru.

Raised by Indrabodhi, king of Oḍḍiyāna, Padmasambhava left home as a young man. After obtaining ordi-
nation from the Buddha's close disciple Ānanda, he
traveled through all realms, manifesting in different
forms to receive teachings and demonstrate perfection. Having attained immortality, he came to Tibet in
the eighth century of the present era. Here, in fulfill-
ment of a vow made in a previous lifetime, he worked
together with King Khri-srong lDe'u-btsan and the
abbot Śāntarakṣita to establish the Dharma. Training
twenty-five disciples in the inner Tantras at bSam-yas
and mChims-phu, he directed the concealment of
thousands of texts for recovery, at times when they
would be most effective and beneficial. It is said that
Padmasambhava remained in Tibet for 111 years
before departing to aid beings in other realms.

Nāgārjuna Prophesied in the Mañjuśrīmūla-tantra,
Nāgārjuna was born in Vidharbha in southern India.
He was expected to live only ten days, but by virtue of
his father's pious actions, his life was extended to
seven years. Sent from home in company of a servant

by his parents, who could not bear to see his death, Nāgārjuna went to the great monastery of Nālandā, where he was healed through practices given him by the abbot Rāhulabhadra. Rāhulabhadra took him as his disciple and ordained him into the Sangha At Nālandā, Nagārjuna became a renowned scholar, accepted as a great master by all Buddhist schools.

Nāgārjuna focused in particular on the teachings of the Prajñāpāramitā. He descended to the realm of the nāgas to obtain the Prajñāpāramitā in 100,000 lines, which had been given to the nāgas for safekeeping. Having mastered these profound teachings, he explicated the doctrine of śūnyatā and the meaning of the Middle Way in a series of commentaries. His teachings became a central inspiration of all followers of the Mahāyāna, and his works provided the foundation of the Mādhyamika school. Together with Asaṅga, he is known as one of the two Most Excellent Ones of India.

Āryadeva The chief disciple of Nāgārjuna, Āryadeva continued the work of his master and further explicated his teachings on the Middle way. Miraculously born from a great lotus in Sinhaladvīpa (modern Sri Lanka), Āryadeva was raised as heir to the throne but renounced it in favor of a religious life. On a pilgrimage to India, Āryadeva met Nāgārjuna and became his disciple. After Nāgārjuna passed away, Āryadeva built at Śrī Parvata twenty-four monasteries dedicated to the Mahāyāna teachings. He devoted most of his life to writing commentaries on Nāgārjuna's works as well as texts on aspects of the Middle Way. These works, together with those of his master Nāgārjuna, established the foundation for the philosophical tradition that became known as Mādhyamika.

Asaṅga   Asaṅga was born in Puruṣapura (modern Peshawar) in Gandhāra in the northwest. Ordained in his youth, Asaṅga studied the scriptures intensively. For twelve years he meditated in a cave in a mountain south of Rājagṛha, invoking the guidance of Maitreya so that he could deepen his understanding the profound Prajñāpāramitā. When, through an act of selfless compassion, Asaṅga became able to recognize the great Bodhisattva, Maitreya took him to the heaven realms and instructed him for many years. These teachings, written down by Asaṅga, became known as the Five Treatises of Maitreya. Asaṅga devoted the rest of his life to expanding upon these works, which, together with the Abhidharmasamuccaya, Yogacaryā-bhūmi, and other śāstras by Asaṅga and Vasubandhu, became the basis for the Yogācāra tradition.

Asaṅga traveled widely to establish new centers and temples. It is said that nearly all followers of the Mahāyāna throughout India heard him teach and that the number of his disciples could not be counted. He passed away at Rājagṛha, where a stūpa was built to hold his relics. Together, Asaṅga and Nāgārjuna are renowned as the two Most Excellent Ones of India

Vasubandhu   Stated by the Tibetan historian Tāranātha to be a contemporary of King lHa-tho-tho-ri of Tibet, Vasubandhu was Asaṅga's younger brother.

Ordained at Nālandā at an early age, he became expert in the six systems of classical philosophy and is said to have memorized the entire Tripiṭaka. Mastering Abhidharma under the guidance of Buddhamitra, Manorātha, and Sanghabhadra, he systematized the Sarvāstivādin teachings in his verse treatise, the Abhidharmakoṣa-kārikā, then critiqued them from the Sautrāntika viewpoint in his Abhidharmakoṣabhāṣya. These two works took on fundamental importance for all later students of Abhidharma.

Vasubandhu at first rejected the Mahāyāna teachings propounded by Asaṅga, but was converted to the Great Vehicle upon hearing two Sūtras recited by Asaṅga's disciples. He composed numerous commentaries and applied his brilliant intellect to developing the Vijñānavāda doctrine of Vijñaptimātra, expressed in the Viṁśatikā and Triṁśikā Kārikās. He succeeded Asaṅga as abbot of Nālandā and established additional new Mahāyāna centers. It is said that he taught nearly sixty thousand monks, and that his disciples included four outstanding masters: Sthiramati, learned in Abhidharma; Guṇaprabha, learned in Vinaya; Dignāga, expert in logic and epistemology, and Vimuktasena, learned in Prajñāpāramitā.

Dignāga Dignāga was one of the earliest Buddhist logicians. In his writings on logic and epistemology he established proofs for valid knowledge that supported the work of the great Buddhist philosophers and helped maintain the purity of the Buddhadharma. In his later life, he enjoyed the patronage of the king of

Orissa, who sponsored the construction of sixteen large monasteries under Dignāga's direction.

As a direct disciple of Vasubandhu, Dignāga studied the doctrines of Hīnayāna and Mahāyāna schools and was inspired to investigate the nature of knowledge. Building upon Sautrāntika inquiries into perception and cognition, Dignāga analyzed the basis of logical reasoning and developed a comprehensive theory of knowledge. Mañjuśrī appeared to him directly and proclaimed that in the future his work would be the only eye of all the śāstras. During his lifetime, he had no disciple who was his equal in logic; however, his work was continued by his student Īśvarasena, who in turn became the teacher of the great master Dharmakīrti, Dignāga's worthy successor.

Buddhapālita The Mādhyamika master Buddha-pālita was an important commentator on the works of Nāgārjuna and the first to set forth the interpretation that gave rise to the Prāsaṅgika-Mādhyamika school. Born in the southern region of Tambala, he was ordained at an early age. After he had completed a classical education and mastered the teachings of the scriptures, he studied the texts of Nāgārjuna under Sangharakṣita, the disciple of Nāgamitra. In the course of his meditation practice, he had a vision of Mañjuśrī and attained great knowledge through the Bodhi-sattva's blessings. Many of his texts have been lost, but in those that survive he emphasizes Nāgārjuna's use of prasaṅga, a method that draws out the necessary consequences of positions to demonstrate their limits.

Buddhapālita taught Kamalabuddhi, the teacher of Candrakīrti, the great explicator of Prāsaṅgika-mādhyamika. It was Candrakīrti who continued this teaching most strongly and became the master architect of the Prāsaṅgika dialectic.

Bhāvaviveka Known also as Bhavya, Bhāvaviveka was a younger contemporary of Buddhapālita. He founded an alternative school of Mādhyamika known as the Svātantrika-Mādhyamika, a tradition that has continued to flourish to the present day. According to some sources, he was the incarnation of the Buddha's disciple Subhūti.

Born in southern India, Bhāvaviveka studied with Sangharakṣita (also the teacher of Buddhapālita) at the great monastic university of Nālandā. He studied the works of Buddhapālita, and his own views evolved in response. Later in life he returned to southern India, where he was associated with numerous monasteries. In all, he taught thousands of students, who disseminated his teachings widely.

Candrakīrti Born in southern India, Candrakīrti became a scholar widely known for his mastery of the Tripiṭaka. Building on Nāgārjuna's teachings as well as those of his teacher Kamalabuddhi, a student of the renowned master Buddhapālita, he became the foremost proponent of the Prāsaṅgika-mādhyamika tradition. The Prasannapadā, his important commentary on Nāgārjuna's work, has guided countless followers of the Mahāyāna.

At Nālandā, where he served as abbot, Candrakīrti defeated the most prominent tīrthika masters in debate. He also engaged in a series of famous debates with the noted Buddhist master Candragomin, who propounded a different view of Mādhyamika. A highly realized master, Candrakīrti is said to have possessed great psychic powers. Demonstrating the fallacy of distinctions, he provided the Sangha with food in a time of famine by milking a cow painted on a mural. At another time he protected Nālandā by driving away invaders while riding a stone lion. Eventually he returned to southern India, where he spent many years in intensive practice and established large Dharma centers.

Śāntideva   Born to a king in western India, Śāntideva was inspired to renounce his royal status when he had a vision of the Bodhisattva Mañjuśrī seated on his father's throne. As a student at Nālandā University, he presented himself as a lazy monk, interested only in eating and sleeping. When his fellow monks, wishing to have some fun, invited him to give a teaching, he recited the Bodhicaryāvatāra, a verse treatise on the Bodhisattva path that is now one of the most important of all Mahāyāna commentaries. At the conclusion of his recitation, he rose into the air and disappeared.

In later life, Śāntideva became the minister to a king; however, he was criticized for wearing a wooden sword, which he refused to draw from its scabbard. When the king demanded to see it, Śāntideva warned the king to close one eye. When he drew it forth, its brilliance blinded the monarch's open eye. Chastened, the king built twenty Dharma centers in his realm.

Buddhaguhya Ordained at Nālandā, Buddhaguhya became known together with Padmasambhava and Vimalamitra as one of the three greatest masters of the Inner Yoga Tantras. He received teachings directly from the Great Bodhisattvas and studied with many of the most important Vidyādhara lineage holders. Both Tārā and Mañjuśrī advised him to go on retreat at Mt. Kailāsa, high in the Himalayas. While he was practicing there, emissaries from the Tibetan king Khri-srong lDe'u-btsan invited him to Tibet. While choosing to remain on retreat, he passed on to them his teachings, which have been preserved in lineages transmitted to the present day.

Vimalamitra Born in western India, Vimalamitra was a master of the Inner Yoga Tantras. A direct disciple of Śrī Siṁha, he also received important teachings from Buddhaguhya and from his co-disciple, Jñāna-sūtra. He became the most revered among five hundred teachers at the court of the king of Oḍḍiyāna. It was there that emissaries of King Khri-srong lDe'u-btsan found him and invited him to Tibet.

In Tibet, Vimalamitra taught at the court, assisted with the massive translation projects at bSam-yas, and worked with Padmasambhava's twenty-five principal disciples. He taught Atiyoga in secret to the king and a few close disciples and wrote several texts in Tibetan that he concealed for later discovery. After thirteen years he left Tibet to go on retreat at Mt. Wu-t'ai-shan in China, but promised to take rebirth once in each century to help protect the Dharma in Tibet.

Śāntarakṣita   The foremost Buddhist scholar of his time, Śāntarakṣita was born to a royal family in Sahora. Holder of the Vinaya lineage of Rāhula and of all Mahāyāna philosophical traditions, he initiated the Yogācāra-svātantrika-mādhyamika, a system known for integrating and systematizing the most important elements of Mahāyāna philosophical thought.

Invited to Tibet by King Khri-srong lDe'u-btsan, Śāntarakṣita worked together with the king and Guru Padmasambhava to found bSamyas monastery as a home for the Dharma in Tibet. When the monastery was ready, he ordained the first seven Tibetan monks, establishing the Vinaya lineage since followed by all Tibetans. After his death, his disciple Kamalaśīla, acting as his master had instructed, represented the teachings of the Indian masters in a great debate that shaped the course of the Dharma in Tibet for all time.

Haribhadra   A disciple of Śāntarakṣita, Haribhadra is known as the most important commentator on the Prajñāpāramitā Sūtras and their commentary by Maitreya. Inspired by a vision of Maitreya to compose such a commentary, he received support from King Dharmapāla, who invited him to eastern India. Under the influence of Haribhadra, who instructed him in Dharma, the king constructed fifty temples, among them the great monastic university of Vikramaśīla.

Tilopa Originally a monk, Tilopa later became a great siddha, famed for his direct teachings and songs of realization. It is said that as a young man he placed himself in chains for twelve years to manifest his intense desire to meditate without interruption. Transcending limits of space and time, he received teachings from many great masters of the past, and he told his students that he had no teacher in human form. Through his greatest disciple, Nāropa, he passed on the lineage of Mahāmudrā teachings to Tibet.

Nāropa This great master was born to a royal family in Bengal, India in the eleventh century C.E. He studied for three years in Kashmir, then returned home, where he lived as a householder before turning to the Dharma. Resuming his studies in Kashmir and at Pullahari, he eventually came to Nālandā, where his outstanding scholarship earned him the position of abbot.

When a visionary event revealed to him the need for a different kind of knowledge, Nāropa left Nālandā in search of the great siddha Tilopa. Aware that Nāropa was underway, Tilopa accompanied him in secret, assuming various forms to guide his student through twelve experiences, each marked by a sight of unparalleled ugliness, that led him closer to realization. When Nāropa finally met Tilopa, he remained with him for twelve years and received the full transmission of his master's Mahāmudrā teachings. Later, he transmitted them to his Tibetan disciple Mar-pa. Through Mar-pa and Mar-pa's disciple Mi-la-res-pa, these teachings became widely established in Tibet.

Tibetan Masters

Vairotsana (8th–9th centuries)   Vairotsana rakṣita, spiritual son of Padmasambhava, was Tibet's earliest Vidyādhara and most brilliant scholar and translator. He is said to have mastered as many as 360 different dialects. Born into the sPa-gor clan, Vairotsana was sent to India by Khri-srong lDe'u-btsan to study with Indian paṇḍitas and became known from his skill in discourse and practice. He traveled widely and received teachings from more than twenty-five of the greatest Dharma masters of all times. His principal teacher was Śrī Siṁha, from whom he received the instructions and empowerments of all three cycles of the Atiyoga teachings. He attained full realization when Surativajra, emanation of Vajrasattva in human form, appeared to him and gave him the complete Atiyoga texts.

Upon his return to Tibet, Vairotsana became one of the original seven monks to be ordained by Śāntarakṣita. He assisted Vimalamitra and Padmasambhava in teaching and translating. He taught philosophy and the fundamental teachings of the Dharma to Khri-srong lDe'u-btsan and scholars of the court during the day, while at night he transmitted the esoteric Atiyoga teachings to the king and his other close disciples. Unfairly attacked by jealous court ministers, Vairotsana departed for Eastern Tibet, but eventually he was recalled by the king. He translated many of Śrī Siṁha's works and other Mantrayāna texts, as well as important Sūtras.

Ma-rpa Lo-tsā-ba Chos-kyi Blo-gros (1012–1097) At an early age, Mar-pa was inspired to devote his life to translating Buddhist texts. He began to study Sanskrit under the guidance of 'Brog-mi Śākya Ye-shes, then traveled to India, where he became a principal disciple of the great master Nāropa. He returned to India twice more to study and practice the Mantrayāna with Nāropa and others of India's most realized siddhas, including Avadhuti-pa and Nāropa's sister Nigumī, who transmitted to him the six yogas of Nāropa.

Mar-pa's teachings and his translation activities established the foundation for the gSar-ma (new) transmission that brought to Tibet the śāstras of later Indian masters and new Mantrayāna lineages. While Mar-pa had four principal disciples, his lineages continued most strongly through the beloved and highly realized yogin Mi-la-ras-pa.

Mi-la-ras-pa (1040–1123) Mi-la-ras-pa is Tibet's outstanding yogin, poet, and saint, revered and beloved by all Tibetan Buddhist traditions. Obedient to his mother's wishes, he studied magic as a young man and brought about violent rainstorms, ruining those who had impoverished his family. To atone for the suffering incurred, he became Mar-pa's disciple and applied himself to the difficult tasks Mar-pa assigned him. Six years later, freed from his karma through the merit of his devotion, he was able to receive Mar-pa's complete teachings. He attained realization through the practice of Mahāmudrā and the teachings known as the six yogas of Nāropa.

Famed for wearing only a single white cotton robe, Mi-la-ras-pa lived as a recluse while teaching disciples who gathered to hear him. Among them were sGam-po-pa, from whom derive the four major and eight subsidiary schools of the Kagyud tradition, and Ras-chung-pa, who took over responsibility for the disciples after Mi-la-ras-pa passed away at the age of eighty-four. His teachings, expressed in inspiring songs of realization, remain a living legacy meaningful to all Buddhist practitioners.

Sa-chen Kun-dga' sNying-po (1092–1158)   The son of 'Khon dKon-mchog rGyal-po, disciple of 'Brog-mi Lo-tsā-ba and founder of Sa-skya monastery, Sa-chen Kun-dga' sNying-po was regarded from an early age as an emanation of Mañjuśrī. His later life confirmed his predisposition to outstanding scholarship, dedication to the education of disciples, and commitment to the Bodhisattva ideal. From 'Brog-mi he received the complete transmission lineage of the Lam-'bras (Path and Fruit) teachings. As abbot of Sa-skya monastery he consolidated and enlarged the Sa-skya school. His work was continued by his two sons, bSod-nams rTse-mo and Grags-pa rGyal-mtshan, the father of Sa-skya Paṇḍita. Sa-chen and his sons are also known as the Three White Masters of the Sa-skya school, while Sa-skya Paṇḍita and his nephew 'Phags-pa are known as the Two Red Masters. Collectively, they are revered as the Five Great Venerables.

Sa-skya Paṇḍita Kun-dga' rGyal-mtshan (1182–1251)
Kun-dga' rGyal-mtshan, renowned as Sa-skya Paṇḍita,

master logician and the greatest scholar of the Sa-skya school, won the respect of Tibetans and Mongolians alike for his work on behalf of the Dharma. Descended from 'Khon dKon-mchog rGyal-po, the founder of Sa-skya monastery, he became the disciple of the Kashmiri paṇḍita Śākyaśrī, who had recently come to Tibet. In collaboration with Śākyaśrī, he translated Dharmakīrti's Pramāṇavārttika, one of the most important Buddhist texts on logic. Excelling in all branches of knowledge, he became a renowned scholar and logician, considered to have no equal in debate in the whole of India and Tibet.

Klong-chen Rab-'byams-pa (1308–1364) Klong-chen Rab-'byams-pa, one of the few Tibetan masters to bear the title kun-mkhyen (all-knowing), exemplifies the heart of the Nyingma tradition. He is regarded as an incarnation of Mañjuśrī, emanation of enlightened wisdom, and also of Vimalamitra, the paṇḍita from Oḍḍiyāna who contributed greatly to the early transmission of Buddhism in Tibet. He received the complete transmission of the Mahā, Anu, and Atiyoga lineages, as well as the sNying-thig, the most precious distillation of the esoteric teachings. Like sacred relics, his teachings were treasured for their ability to uplift and inspire, opening the eye of insight and enabling students to comprehend the most profound truths. They include the texts known as the mDzod-bdun, or Seven Treasures, and three renowned trilogies.

Klong-chen-pa spent ten years in Bhutan, where he founded monasteries from which the rDzogs-chen teachings were later brought to Nepal. Returning to Tibet, he strengthened several monastic settlements and restored the monastery of bSam-yas before entering his final retreat in Padmasambhava's meditation cave at mChims-phu.

Rig-'dzin rGod-ldem-can (1337–1409) Rig-'dzin rGod-ldem is renowned as the discoverer of the Byang-gter, or Northern Treasures, an important collection of powerful gTer-ma. The teachings he mastered, explicated, and transmitted formed the basis of a distinctive rDzogs-chen system that has continued to the present day.

Guided by his father, the siddha bDud-'dul, Rig-'dzin rGod-ldem studied and practiced Nyingma teachings from childhood. Following a list of treasures received from another gTer-ston, he recovered numerous gTer-ma and devoted his life to making them available to his disciples and future generations. Among his most important contributions is a text summarizing the distilled essence of the rNying-ma rGyud-'bum. The teachings he revealed have been transmitted to the present by an unbroken lineage of realized siddhas, including his son, his consort, and the reincarnation of rGod-ldem-can himself.

Sangs-rgyas Gling-pa (1340–1396) Ordained at an early age, Sangs-rgyas Gling-pa was recognized as exceptional by his root teacher, the great Karmapa Rol-pa'i rDo-rje, who prophesied that he would guide many living beings to liberation. Inspired by a vision of Guru Padmasambhava, he recovered the treasure teachings known as Bla-ma-dgongs-'dus, which he divided into thirteen volumes. Twenty streams of transmission flowed from this work alone. He went on to discover at least eighteen more treasure troves, teachings that spread most strongly in eastern Tibet and later took root in Bhutan, where they remain vital today. In the fifteenth century, the fifth Karmapa carried some of them to China and presented them to the Ming emperor.

Sangs-rgyas Gling-pa founded bDe-chen bSam-grub monastery. His disciples included his own teacher, Karmapa Rol-pa'i rDo-rje, Zhwa-dmar Karmapa mKha'-spyod dBang-po, and other illustrious lamas.

Tsong-kha-pa (1357–1419) Tripiṭaka master and scholar, rJe Tsong-kha-pa became a monk at an early age and throughout his life strongly upheld the monastic tradition. Considered by many to be an incarnation of the Indian master Atiśa, he received Atiśa's bKa'-gdams lineages and studied the major gSar-ma Tantras under Sa-skya and bKa'-brgyud masters. He also received teachings from the Nyingma siddha Legs-gyi rDo-rje and the Zha-lu master Chos-kyi dPal. In 1409, at his monastery at dGa'-ldan, he established the New bKa'-gdams tradition. It became the basis for the Gelugpa school, based on the teachings of Atiśa, which emphasized the study of Vinaya, the Tripiṭaka, and the śastras. Tsong-kha-pa strengthened the Sangha and introduced strict monastic reforms. He composed the Lam-rim Chen-mo, an explanation of the Mahāyāna path that served as the root teaching for the new school. He also composed numerous summaries of the fundamental teachings of the Buddhist philosophical schools as well as important commentaries on Vinaya and Prajñāpāramitā, Candrakīrti's Madhyamakāvatāra, logic and epistemology, and the gSar-ma Tantras, and encouraged the application of logic in formal debates. His lineages were transmitted vigorously by disciples who established major monasteries in Mongolia and China as well as in Tibet. Among them was dGe-'dun Grub, the First Dalai Lama.

Ratna Gling-pa (1403–1479)   The great gTer-ston Ratna Gling-pa, reincarnation of one of Padmasambhava's twenty-five principal disciples, mastered all fields of Buddhist learning. He recovered so many concealed treasures that he is said to have completed the work of three lifetimes.

Ratna Gling-pa figures prominently in the bKa'-ma transmission of the Nyingma Tantras. At a time when copies of these Tantras were rare and dispersed throughout Tibet, he obtained the oral transmission of these teachings from the last living master to hold them. Collecting the texts, he compiled them into the rNying-ma rGyud-'bum, the Hundred Thousand rNying-ma Tantras, which survives today in several editions. Ratna Gling-pa's disciples were said to fill Tibet from Mount Kailāsa in the west to rGyal-mo-rong in the east. His principal disciples were his four Heart Sons. The lineages they transmitted have come down unbroken to the present day, along with more than one thousand texts by Ratna Gling-pa himself.

mNga'-ris Paṇ-chen Padma dBang-rgyal (1487–1542) Born in Nepal, Padma dBang-rgyal received teachings in the bKa'-ma from his father, a disciple of Mar-pa. He received teachings in Vinaya and Sūtra from Norbstan bzang-po and took the Bodhisattva vows under the guidance of his father. By the age of twenty, he was already a master of Madhyamaka, epistemology and logic, and Prajñāpāramitā. He received the Lam-'bras (Path and Fruit) teachings as well as tantric empowerments, and studied and practiced the gTer-mas known as the Northern Treasures.

Resolved to help restore the teachings in central Tibet, Padma dBang-rgyal went to lHa-sa, where he received inspiring prophecies, and to bSam-yas, where he recalled his former existence as King Khri-srong lDe'u-btsan. He met and received teachings from numerous eminent masters, restored the Dharma traditions of lHo-brag monastery, and together with other masters reconsecrated the great monastery of bSam-yas. At bSam-yas, he recovered sādhanas for the teachings known as the Prayer in Seven Chapters and composed an important treatise on the three vows of Hīnayāna, Mahāyāna, and Vajrayāna.

Lo-chen Dharmaśrī (1654–1717) In the seventeenth century, when the Nyingma lineages were weakening, they were revitalized and preserved through the efforts of two outstanding masters: the great gTer-ston

O-rgyan gTer-bdag Gling-pa and his younger brother Lo-chen Dharmaśrī. Ordained by the Fifth Dalai Lama, Lo-chen Dharmaśrī excelled in philosophical studies as well as in the classical disciplines of language, arts, and sciences. From his brother, his root teacher, he received the lineages of the bKa'-ma and gTer-ma teachings transmitted through Klong-chen-pa and other major Nyingma masters. In all, he received teachings from twenty-two of the greatest masters of his day. Applying the three methods of teaching, debate, and composition, he taught continuously, conveying the scope of the Dharma to a wide range of disciples and students at sMin-grol-gling monastery. The range of his knowledge is expressed in more than two hundred texts, including major commentaries on Tantra, philosophy, ritual, and poetics. Although his monastery was destroyed during the Mongol invasion, his work established the foundation of the sMin-gling lineage, a major stream of transmission that continues to the present day.

Dwags-po-bKra-shis rNam-rgyal (16th–17th century)
A disciple of Ngag-gi dBang-po, a Dharma master of the Northern gTer-ma Treasures, bKra-shis rNam-rgyal composed a brilliant work clarifying the tenets of the Nyingma school. This work has come down to the present day.

dGe-rtse Mahāpaṇḍita (fl. 1764)   The great Nyingma scholar 'Gyur-med Tshe-dbang mChog-grub, generally known as Kaḥ-thog dGer-tse Mahāpaṇḍita, consolidated the foundation for Nyingma scholarship by cataloging the sDe-dge edition of the rNying-ma rGyud-'bum. Working at Kaḥ-thog monastery, he also composed a commentary on the root Mahāyoga Tantra, a treatise on a text by Padmasambhava on the significance of the Mantrayāna, and other works that have come down to the present time.

'Jigs-med Gling-pa (1730–1798) Born in central Tibet, 'Jigs-med Gling-pa belonged to a stream of incarnations including the great master Klong-chen-pa (fourteenth century). From Klong-chen-pa he received visionary blessings and the teachings of the Klong-chen-snying-thig cycle. His principal residence was Tshe-ring-ljongs Padma 'Od-gsal Theg-mchog Gling, an ancient hermitage that he had rebuilt. His disciples included masters of all the Tibetan schools, who came to him from every region of Tibet. As a result of his activities, the precious instructions of the Klong-chen-snying-thig spread widely and their practices have remained vital to the present day.

dPal-sprul Rinpoche (1808–1887) An incarnation of 'Jigs-med Gling-pa and also of the renowned Indian paṇḍita Śāntideva, dPal-sprul Rinpoche was famed for his profound understanding of Śāntideva's teachings on the Bodhisattva view and path. From his teachers he received Klong-chen-pa's sNying-thig (Heart-drop) lineage as transmitted by 'Jigs-med Gling-pa. He transmitted both of these precious lineages to A-'dzom 'Brug-pa in gratitude for A-'dzom's compassion in guiding his mother's consciousness at the time of her death. dPal-sprul was a Dharma brother and contemporary of the great 'Jam-dbyangs mKhyen-brtse, and both masters were pivotal in strengthening the Dharma traditions of Tibet and influencing future generations of teachers to follow their example. For most of his life, dPal-sprul lived as a wandering yogin. His teachings continue to inspire and guide Dharma students today.

'Jam-mgon Kong-sprul Blo-gros mTha'-yas (1813–1899)   Born in Khams, 'Jam-mgon Kong-sprul, an incarnation of Vairotsana, received a traditional training in the classical arts and sciences and the Sūtrayāna texts. Working with fifty other masters, he accumulated teachings from all of the eight practice lineages. Dudjom Rinpoche wrote that his life was like four lifetimes condensed into one: as a writer, a teacher, a practitioner, and sponsor of monastic communities, sacred art, and renovation projects. A highly accomplished master of the Tibetan language, Kong-sprul composed hundreds of texts, which were compiled into collections known as the Five Treasures.

Together with 'Jam-dbyangs mKhyen-brtse and his foremost disciple, mChog-gyur Gling-pa, Kong-sprul discovered numerous treasures and collected many more discovered previously, compiling them into the Rin-chen gTer-mdzod.

'Jam-dbyangs mKhyen-brtse dBang-po (1820–1892)
'Jam-dbyangs mKhyen-brtse dBang-po, renowned as the fifth gTer-ston King, was an incarnation of 'Jigmed Gling-pa and King Khri-srong lDe'u-bstan. Born

near sDe-dge, he was ordained by Rig-'dzin bZang-po, abbot of sMin-grol-gling. He studied with one hundred and fifty tantric and academic scholars, mastered all fields of philosophy and the teaching of the eight practice lineages, and received the lineages of both rNying-ma and gSar-ma Tantras.

'Jam-dbyangs mKhyen-brtse held all Seven Streams of the Nyingma teachings. Together with mChog-gyur Gling-pa and 'Jam-mgon Kong-sprul Blo-gros mTha'-yas, he discovered many concealed gTer-ma texts, including Earth Treasures as well as the rare and precious teachings known as the Realization Treasures, Pure Vision Treasures, and Hearing Treasures.

Kun-bzang dPal-ldan (early 19th–mid 19th century) An outstanding scholar who lived in eastern Tibet, Kun-bzang dPal-ldan received teachings from such great masters as dPal-sprul Rinpoche, Lama Mi-pham, and Kaḥ-thog Si-tu. He served as abbot at the college for philosophical studies at Kaḥ-thog monastery, and instructed Bod-pa Tulku, 'Jam-dbyangs mKhyen-brtse Chos-kyi Blo-gros, Nus-ldan, and Ngag-chung—masters who were themselves renowned as great teachers and writers. Among his writings were a biography of Lama Mi-pham and commentaries on the Yon-tan-mdzod and the Bodhicaryāvatāra.

A-'dzom 'Brug-pa (1842–1924) A-'dzom 'Brug-pa began preliminary practices under the guidance of Kaḥ-thog Si-tu, who recognized his exceptional meditative abilities and sent him to study with the great

'Jam-dbyangs mKhyen-brtse dBang-po. Following this master's direction, he became a gTer-ston and discovered hidden teachings that have been transmitted to the present day. He received transmission of the entire Rin-chen gTer-mdzod from 'Jam-mgon Kong-sprul Blo-gros mTha'-yas, and he was a close friend of the famed Lama Mi-pham. A renowned Atiyoga teacher, he composed at least 148 texts and exchanged initiations with numerous masters of his time. His major disciples were his sons, 'Gyur-med rDo-rje and Padma dBang-rgyal, who continued his lineages.

Lama Mi-pham (1846–1912)   Mi-pham 'Jam-dbyangs rNam-rgyal rGya-mtsho, generally known as Lama Mi-pham, studied with dPal-sprul Rinpoche, 'Jam-dbyangs mKhyen-brtse, Kong-sprul, and other outstanding scholars and practitioners. Lama Mi-pham's knowledge spanned the entire spectrum of classical and technical studies. He composed thirty-five volumes on such diverse topics as logic, philosophy, astrology, cosmology, painting, sculpture, engineering, chemistry, medicine, meditation, and Tantra. His most famous works include a commentary on the ninth chapter of the Bodhicaryāvatāra, a Tibetan-Sanskrit dictionary for specialized rDzogs-chen terms, a commentary on Sanskrit aesthetics, and transcriptions of the oral Gesar epic. He transmitted his knowledge and lineages to numerous great masters.

gZhan-dga' (gZhan-phan Chos-kyi sNang-ba) (1871–1927)   gZhan-phan Chos-kyi sNang-ba, also known as mKhan-po gZhan-dga', was apreceptor of Siṁha

College at rDzogs-chen monastery. From his principal teacher bsTan-'dzin Nor-bu, a direct disciple of dPal-sprul Rinpoche, he gained a comprehensive understanding of the Mahāyāna philosophical traditions. He spent the greater part of his life teaching the śāstras in eastern Tibet. In support of the curriculum he established for his students, he composed commentaries on thirteen fundamental śāstras by the great Indian commentators, a non-sectarian collection relied on today in the Nyingma, Kagyud, and Sakya schools.

Kaḥ-thog Situ Chos-kyi rGya-mtsho (1880–1925)
Kaḥ-thog Situ was a disciple of the first 'Jam-dbyangs mKhyen-brtse and Lama Mi-pham and the teacher of the second 'Jam-dbyangs mKhyen-brtse, Chos-kyi Blo-gros. Early in his career, he received the sMin-grol-gling Vinaya and Bodhisattva lineages as well as the sNying-thig lineage of Klong-chen-pa, and transmitted teachings to the finest scholars of central Tibet. His guides for pilgrimage to holy places and writings on the stupas of Nepal are respected by all traditions. To honor Padmasambhava, he rebuilt the Great Guru's Copper Mountain monument at Kaḥ-thog. He created a curriculum of Dharma study based on one hundred essential Sūtras, śāstras, and Tantras.

Kaḥ-thog Situ recovered several major lost teachings, including an Anuyoga commentary by gNubs-chen Sangs-rgyas Ye-shes and the bKa'-mchims-phu-ma, Padmasambhava's own commentary on the gSang-ba'i-snying-po Tantra. His library was widely recognized as one of the treasures of Tibet.

Fifty-One Mental Events

FIVE OMNIPRESENT EVENTS

Feeling	vedanā	tshor-ba
Perception	samjñā	'du-shes
Intention	cetanā	sems-pa
Contact	sparśa	reg-pa
Attention	manaskāra	yid la byed-pa

FIVE OBJECT-DETERMINING EVENTS

Interest	chanda	'dun-pa
Determination	adhimokṣa	mos-pa
Mindfulness	smṛti	dran-pa
Concentration	samādhi	ting-nge-'dzin
Discernment	prajñā	shes-rab

ELEVEN VIRTUOUS MENTAL EVENTS

Faith	śraddhā	dad-pa
Conscientiousness	apramāda	bag-yod
Alert Ease	praśrabdhi	shin-tu sbyangs-pa
Equanimity	upekṣā	btang-snyoms
Self-respect	hrī	ngo-tsha
Propriety	apatrāpya	khrel yod-pa
Nonattachment	alobha	ma chags-pa
Nonaversion	adveṣa	zhe-sdang med-pa

Effort	vīrya	brtson-'grus
Nonviolence	avihiṁsā	rnam-parmi-'tshe-ba
Nonconfusion	amoha	gti-mug med-pa

Six Basic Emotions

Desire	rāga	'dod-chags
Anger	pratigha	khong-khro
Pride	māna	nga-rgyal
Ignorance	avidyā	ma-rig-pa
Doubt	vicikitsā	the-tshoms
Opinionatedness	dṛṣti	lta-ba

Twenty Proximate Factors of Instability

Vindictiveness	krodha	khro-ba
Resentment	upanāha	khon-du 'dzin-pa
Spite	pradāśa	'tshig-pa
Malice	vihiṁsā	rnam-par 'tshe-ba
Jealousy	īrṣyā	phrag-dog
Dishonesty	śāṭhya	g.yo
Deceit	māya	sgyu
Hypocrisy	mrakṣa	'chab-pa
Avarice	mātsarya	ser-sna
Haughtiness	mada	rgyags-pa
Lack of self-respect	āluīkya	ngo-tsha med-pa
Lack of propriety	anapatrāpya	khrel med-pa
Torpor	styāna	rmugs-pa

Restlessness	auddhyata	rgod-pa
Faithlessness	āśraddhya	ma-dad-pa
Laziness	kausīdya	le-lo
Nonconscientiousness	pramāda	bag-med
Forgetfulness	muṣitasmṛtitā	brjed ngas-pa
Inattentiveness	asamprajanya	shes-pa bzhin ma-yin
Distractedness	vikṣepa	rnam-pa g.yeng-ba

FOUR VARIABLES

Worry	kaukṛtya	gyod-pa
Sleepiness	middha	gnyid-pa
Investigation	vitarka	rtog-pa
Analysis	vicāra	dpyod-pa

The Eight Forms of Sangha

monk	bhikṣu	dge-slong
nun	bhikṣunī	dge-slong-ma
male novice	śramaṇa	dge-tshul
female novice	śramanī	dge-tshul-ma
those too young for ordination	śikṣamana	dge-slob-pa, dge-slob-ma
temporary vow holder	upavastha	
male householder	upasaka	dge-bsnyen-pha
female householder	upasikā	dge-bsnyen-ma

The Thirteen Śāstras Identified by gZhan-dga'

Prātimokṣa Sūtra, So-sor thar-pa'i mdo, by Śākyamuni Buddha

Vinayasūtra, 'Dul-ba'i-mdo-rtsa-ba, by Guṇaprabha

Abhidharmakoṣabhāsya, Chos-mngon-pa'i-mdzod-tshig-le'ur-byas-pa, by Vasubandhu

Abhidharma-samuccaya, Chos-mngon-pa-kun-las btus pa, by Asaṅga

Mūlamadhyamakakārikā, dBu-ma-rtsa-ba'i-tshig-le'ur-byas-pa, by Nāgārjuna

Catuḥśataka, dBu-ma-bzhi-brgya-pa, by Āryadeva

Madhyamakāvatāra, dBu-ma-la-'jug-pa, by Candrakīrti

Bodhicaryāvatāra, Byang-chub-sems-dpa'i-spyod-pa-la-'jug-pa, by Śāntideva

Abhisamayālaṃkāra, mNgon-par rtogs-pa'i-rgyan, by Maitreya

Mahāyānasūtrālaṃkāra, Theg-pa-chen-po-mdo-sde'i-rgyan, by Maitreya

Madhyāntavibhaṅga   dBus-dang-mtha'-rnam-par-'byed-pa, by Maitreya

Dharmadharmatāvibhaṅga   Chos-dang-chos-nyid-nam-par-'byed-pa, by Maitreya

Mahāyānottaratantra (Uttaratantra), Theg-pa-chen-po-rgyud-bla-ma, by Maitreya

Index

About the Author

Tarthang Tulku is an accomplished Tibetan lama raised
in Tibet who has lived and
worked in the United States
since 1969. Ever since leav-
ing Tibet, he has dedicated
his full energy and resources
to preserving and transmitting the Dharma.

In the early 1960s, while teaching at Sanskrit
University in Vārāṇasī, Tarthang Tulku founded
Dharma Mudrānālaya Press and began publishing
texts he had brought with him from Tibet. In 1971,
soon after arriving in America, he established Dharma
Publishing and Dharma Press. He is also founder of
the Nyingma Institute in Berkeley and its affiliated
centers, where several thousand students have come
in contact with the Buddhist teachings, as well as
founder and creator of Odiyan Buddhist Center and
Ratna Ling, country centers for Dharma work, retreats,
study, and translation.

An active author and educator, Tarthang Tulku
has written eighteen books presenting teachings for
the modern world, overseen translations of several
Buddhist texts from the Tibetan, and directed the pro-
duction of the *Nyingma Edition of the bKa'-'gyur and*

bsTan-'gyur. Since 1986, he has guided the creation of *Great Treasures of Ancient Teachings*, the first compilation of a Nyingma Canon together with works by masters of all Tibetan Buddhist traditions. Tarthang Tulku also serves in the traditional role of teacher for a small community of Western students. Always willing to experiment, he has established a form of practice for his students in which their work on behalf of the Dharma becomes a path to realization.

Books in English by Tarthang Tulku

Dynamics of Time and Space
Gesture of Balance
Hidden Mind of Freedom
Invitation to Enlightenment
Knowledge of Freedom
Knowledge of Time and Space
Kum Nye Relaxation
Love of Knoweldge
Mastering Successful Work
Mind over Matter
Openness Mind
Reflections of Mind
Sacred Dimensions of Time and Space
Skillful Means
Teachings from the Heart
Tibetan Relaxation
Time, Space, and Knowledge
Visions of Knowledge

Books by Tarthang Tulku have been translated into sixteen languages: Bulgarian, Chinese, Czech, Dutch,

Estonian, French, German, Hungarian, Italian, Japanese, Korean, Latvian, Polish, Portuguese, Russian, and Spanish. Exclusive of excerpts prepared for college readers, they have been adopted for use in close to a thousand college and university classes, including classes at Boston University, Harvard University, Northwestern University, Pace University, Skidmore College, Stanford School of Business, Swarthmore College, University of Colorado, University of Georgia, and the University of California.

About Dharma Publishing

Dharma Publishing, a non-profit publishing house founded by Tarthang Tulku in 1971, preserves the written teachings and art of the Tibetan Buddhist tradition and produces books that demonstrate the relevance of these teachings to our times. Preservation efforts have led to the publication of the 120-volume *Nyingma Edition of the Tibetan Buddhist Canon* in 1981 and the ongoing preparation of *Great Treasures of Ancient Teachings*, a compendium of more than thirty-one thousand titles by 404 Nyingma masters, 240 authors of other schools, and 128 Indian panditas in nearly seven hundred atlas-size bound volumes. To further support Tibetans displaced from their homelands and seeking to rebuild their culture, more than twelve hundred texts have been typeset and printed in traditional, loose-leaf Tibetan volumes and now in Western-style books. As of 2005, over a million copies of these volumes have been donated to Tibetans in

Asia, together with nearly a million sacred images essential for traditional practice. Additional volumes are prepared and distributed each year.

Dharma Publishing's books in English, more than a hundred titles in all, offer the benefits of Tibet's twelve centuries of research into the human mind, presenting knowledge that supports our highest aspirations for happiness, meaning, and truth. These books are published in eight major series:

Tibetan Translation Series The inspiring works of great masters of the Dharma, starting with the Buddha and continuing to modern times, are timeless in their insights. From accounts of the Buddha's previous lives and biographies of accomplished teachers to detailed instructions on how to follow a spiritual path and practice meditation, these books are the masterpieces of a great civilization, rich in warmth, wit, and wisdom.

Nyingma Psychology Series The word 'Nyingma' means 'Ancient Ones.' While these books are written to relieve the stresses of modern Western life, their insights are rooted in techniques proved valid through the ages. They focus on meditation, increasing awareness, self-healing, and cultivating meaningful activity.

Crystal Mirror Series The light of the Buddha's teachings illuminated the far reaches of Asia. This series chronicles the teachings in their homeland of India, in Tibet, and throughout Asia. Featuring both original artwork and reproductions, timelines, maps, charts, and glossaries, these volumes present basic

Buddhist teachings, history, and culture with clarity and insight.

Art, History, and Culture Series   Tibetan art has the power to awaken appreciation and convey meaning through symbols that activate subtle dimensions of consciousness. This series explores the significance of sacred art and architecture, the rich history of Tibetan civilization, and the ongoing efforts of the Tibetan people in exile to preserve their priceless legacy.

Dharma in the West Series   The transmission of Buddhism to a new culture offers challenges as well as great potential for benefit and transformation. The works in this series offer insights into the prospects for Western Buddhism and for the interaction of Buddhism with the emerging global culture. They explore points of contact, the danger of misunderstanding, and approaches suited to these times and circumstances.

Time, Space, and Knowledge Series   The TSK vision of reality, presented for the first time in the writings of Tarthang Tulku, takes readers to the boundaries of the known and then beyond. These volumes invite unexpected possibilities, invoking a new vision of self, world, and reality.

Skillful Means Series   Books in the Skillful Means series celebrate and deepen the American work ethic by presenting efficient, productive work as a vehicle for developing spiritual values. Based on Nyingma teachings that unify awareness, concentration, and energy, Skillful Means volumes empower individuals with ways to fearlessly engage the current of daily life and derive meaning from all they do.

Jataka Tales for Children   The Jatakas are accounts of the Buddha's previous lives that convey universal values of friendship, cooperation, non-violence, and patience. Retold for children and young people of all ages, they provide uplifting models and encourage ethical, caring action.

More information available at dharmapublishing.com